Gaelic N

Politics of the Gaelic language
Ireland in the 20th Century

Vincent McKee

First published 1997 by
THE BLUESTACK PRESS
Irish World House
934 North Circular Road
London NW2 7JX

ISBN 1 902147 00 6

Cataloguing information for this title is available from the British Library

Typesetting by The Bluestack Press
Printed in the UK by Marva Print Centre

CONTENTS

DEDICATION

In fond memory and admiration of two outstanding Gaels who brought great respect and honour to the reputation of the Gael during their lives.

I ndil cuimhne agus omois beirt sar Ghael a thus ardmheas agus onoir ar chlu na nGael i rith a saoil.

His Eminence Cardinal Tomas O'Fiaich

Gaelic scholar, Arch-Bishop of Armagh and Primate of All-Ireland 1977-90.

A shoilse an Cairdineal Tomas O'Fiaich

Scholaire sa Ghaeilge, Ard-Easpag Ard Mhacha agus Priomhaidh na hEireann, 1977-90.

and

Right Honourable Donald Steward MP

Former Provost of Stornoway, Scottish Nationalist Member for the Western Isles 1970-87, and Scottish Gaeldom's persistent advocate at Westminster.

An Fior Urranach Domhnall Stiubhart, BP

a bha na Phrobost de Steornabhagh; Ball Baiseanga Albannach airson nan Eilean Sair, 1970-87; Dian thagraiche Gaidhealtachd na h-Alba aig Westminster.

May the light of Heaven shine upon them both.

I solas na bhflaitheas go raibh siad.

ABOUT THE AUTHOR....

Dr Vincent McKee, 39, is from Castlewellan, Co Down, in Northern Ireland.
In 1977 he moved to Coventry, England, as a student and has remained there since.

He is a lecturer and is currently Senior Politics Tutor with the National Extension College, Cambridge and is a regular contributor to a number of newspapers and journals including The Irish News, Parliamentary Affairs and Politics Review.

He has also been a visiting Professor at the University of Santo Tomas, Manila, Philippines and is considered an expert on factionalism within the British party system, having published many research papers on related subjects.

Dr McKee has recently begun work on a history of factionalism in the British Conservative Party since 1945.

His interest in Celtic cultural nationalism and regionalism reflects partly a broad perspective on political developments and partly a life-long personal attachment to Gaelic causes.

In his spare time, McKee enjoys refereeing Gaelic games among the English Midlands ex-patriate Irish community. He also has a particular love for the ballad music of Scottish Gaels and an affinity with the culture of both Gaelic nations.

This is his first book.

PREFACE AND ACKNOWLEDGEMENTS

The stimulus for this book came from reading Reg Hindley's 1990 publication, Death of the Irish Language: A Qualified Obituary.

While genuinely impressed by the comprehensive scope and scholarly nature of Dr Hindley's inquiry, nevertheless I regretted that its conclusions were likely to be of most use to the opponents of the Gaelic language in both Ireland and Scotland.

Its worst thrust was to depress the efforts of Gaeilgeoiri everywhere. Worse; Dr Hindley's book might serve to confirm prejudices already held by anglophile establishments of Scotland and Northern Ireland, and be used to deny Gaeldom its equitable share of funding and other entitlements.

Conversely I felt that something more positive was required, in terms of providing an account of Gaeldom's historic and contemporary developments in Scotland and Northern Ireland throughout the 20th Century.

Moreover, in view of the wide range of other lobbies and causes profiled by sympathetic observers (trade unions, political parties, feminist movements etc) it seems appropriate for Scottish and Ulster Gaeldom's course to be analysed by one holding a natural affinity with its language and culture. That said, this book endeavours to observe all necessary standards of academic inquiry required of a creditable study. While sympathetic to the aims of the Gaeilgeoiri in Scotland and Northern Ireland, I would not allow it to descend into a polemic.

The book is essentially a work of political assessment, rather than a linguistic, sociological or lexographical study. Thus is to be hoped that readers will take an understanding view of the shortcomings that might otherwise appear were this author a Celtic scholar, rather than a political scientist.

This book is concerned with analysing the impact of Gaelicism in the political environments of the two countries, bringing out points of comparison and contrast, and drawing conclusions. In particular, it contrasts the regionalism and relatively apolitical character of modern Scottish Gaeldom with the highly politicised character of Ulster Gaeldom, with the latter having been forced into an historic alliance with Irish Nationalism.

The book attempts mapping out the ever-expanding scope of Gael Uladh; inclusive of language developments, Irish medium schools, the new Belfast Gaeltacht and general culture of Gaelic sports, music and related activities that are embedded in the identity of Northern Nationalists.

Such basic knowledge would be well imparted not just to people outside of Ireland, but also to a readership in the twenty six counties where there appears to be an inadequate appreciation of the restrictive conditions, sturdy and worthy efforts and achievements of Ulster Gaels on various fronts.

Regarding Scotland, the book endeavours to bridge the communication gap by presenting a contemporary picture analysis of the evolving social, educational and cultural infra-structure of Gaidheal Albannaich. The essence of this portrayal is all the more important for the sake of understanding in Ireland and elsewhere, given Scottish Gaeldom's generally low profile outside Scotland.

It is to be hoped that with the advent of a European watchdog catering for minority language/cultural communities, there will be greater awareness of their presence and contributions to the plurality of cultures characterising modern Europe. Specifically, it is essential that such an understanding transcends the Celtic nations to embrace the wider community of European peoples.

Perhaps in the near future there will emerge a plethora of books from scholars across Europe charting the experience of minority peoples and their languages throughout the continent?

In the mean time hopefully this humble effort with all its limitations, for which I accept sole and full responsibility, shall set the ball rolling in the direction of understanding.

I trust it may engender among readers of all persuasions and nationalities an appreciation of the historic and contemporary worlds of the Gaelic nation in both its territories. That much impact will have made this effort worthwhile.

Grateful thanks are due to many people who kindly assisted me with this venture. They include all interviewees listed, as well as the administrative staffs of An Comunn Gaidhealach and Comunn na Gaidhlig (both Inverness), Comhairle Nan Eilean (Stornoway), La (Belfast), N.I. Social Democratic and Labour Party, Newry and Mourne Council, County Down.

Also the politics subject librarian at London Guildhall University Library was helpful with obtaining books on loan and keeping specialist titles for my exclusive attention.

Gratitude is further extended to the following people, who provided various forms of special assistance with materials, advice and presentational support:

Miss Joanne Graham (CNG), Mrs Katie McGregor (retired CNG), Calum MacDonald (ACG), Keith Scammell, Peadar Morgan, Gavin Barrie (Scottish Office), Miss Marie Andrews (Culturlann, Belfast), Peadar MacMuiris & Cathail O'Donnaighle, Noel Doran (Deputy Editor, Irish News), Kathleen Bell (Irish News librarian), Fred Silver and Rod Huckbody (Stornoway Gazette), Terence Bowman and Patrick O'Hare (Mourne Observer), Mrs Geraldine Cosgrove (SDLP General Secretary), Martin O'Brien (BBC Northern Ireland), Miss Sighle Nic An Ultaigh, Maolcholaim Scott, Dr Iain Henderson (Coventry University), Professor James Kellas (Glasgow University), Miss Joanne Murray and family, Michael and Mrs Donella Bartlett, Simon MacKenzie and Donald and Mrs Seonag Maciver (all Lewis and Harris).

Additionally the following persons assisted with my work in a major way, often at great inconvenience and occasional expense to themselves, but always with a generous spirit that is a measure of the personal decency in each of them. Each person brought a special degree of expertise, on which I relied, and for which I was fortunate that our paths met.

Donald John Maciver of Comhairle Nan Eilean, Stornoway, proved my invaluable guide on the comprehensive affairs of Scottish Gaeldom generally and the Gaelic Medium education particularly. His time was freely given in commenting on scripts, offering advice on a variety of related matters, providing materials and statistics, referring me to a useful sources elsewhere in the Gaelic world, and being always available with additional information, translations and such like. I have to add that not only did I come to admire the zeal and knowledge of this great Scottish Gael, but so also did it become apparant over our six-year long friendship that I was dealing with a perfect gentleman.

Dolina MacLeod, Bilingual Development Officer of Comhairle Nan Eilean, also proved most helpful, especially in the early years of my research. Over that period, I was fortunate to have expert advice at short notice on a range of language and cultural affairs, as well as a copious quota of documents, news cuttings and explanations of Council Gaelic policy and programmes. Murdo MacDonald, also a Lewis native, now based in Aberdeen, proved an invaluable aide. His sound knowledge of Hebridean cultural and political affairs, along with a masterful appreciation of the Gaelic language and its social and literary corollaries proved very helpful. His skills as a schoolteacher were put to good effect; it was in a late night discussion with him that the idea for this book came about. More significant was the quiet encouragement which he persistently gave me until the book finally took effect!

On the other side of the Sea of Moyle, I was fortunate to have the pro-active assistance of three leading Gaeilgeoiri. Leading SDLP councillor and policy maker Patsy McGlone, of Cookstown, County Tyrone, was generous with his time and resources, which he shared with me to the full. Patsy provided me with the full range of his contacts, and informed perspective of language developments in Northern society.

Gearoid O'Caireallain, founding Editor of La and current President of Conradh na Gaeilge, was also generous with time, advice and up-to-date primary evidence, as well as comments on parts of the script. So also did Gearoid make available La's photographic library for my use, while facilitating this book with a launch in Belfast on the occasion of Conradh na Gaeilige's Oireachtas '97.

Teacher and Gaeilgeoir, writer and historian, Seamas MacGiolla Fhinnein, proved another invaluable source of help. Seamas made available several primary documents, as well as obtaining copies of old publications and relevant articles, all of which expedited my research. Additionally he assisted with translations, while offering constructive comments on earlier drafts of this book.

It needs adding that this help came in the same generous spirit with which I have always associated Seamas over 27 years of friendship, ever since our schooldays together in County Down.

Another figure meriting grateful acknowledgement is my former Ph.D. supervisor, Professor Tom Nossiter, recently retired from the London School of Economics and Political Science. Over the period of my Doctoral Studies, I was managed by one who is a proven scholar, and also a grand mentor. It was he more than anyone else who guided me in research methods and writing structure, always with a view to maintaining high standards, but also measured by a sensitive regard for developing my style.

I was fortunate to have the guidance of such a fine master at this vital stage of my career. Hence in this, my first book, for which his encouragement was persistent and advice was ever felicitous, I trust in having done some justice to his tutoring standards.

Doubtless time and impressions will tell.

Michelle Mundy, also, should be kindly remembered, for it was she who typed this script for me over many long hours, through night and day.

Thanks to the staff and management of The Bluestack Press, and in particular Paddy McNulty who encouraged this project wholeheartedly, and carried out the typesetting and design.

Finally, I thank my publishing editor, Damien Gaffney, whose confidence in me and patience with all my shortcomings are in need of vindication. Perhaps it is not too ambitious to quietly hope that this book has been worth the wait?

Again, all shortcomings, errors, limitations and inadvertencies are mine, but perhaps amongst the former there might also be occasional merits for the discerning reader. If that proves to be so, then I shall feel the job to have been worthwhile.

Vincent McKee.
Coventry, September 18, 1997.

CHAPTER 1
HISTORICAL BACKGROUND.

Assessments of the politics of contemporary Gaeldom must take account of historic factors relating to the language's decline in both Ireland and Scotland. Moreover, given Gaeldom's broad historic domain embracing all-Ireland and Western Scotland, such assessments must also take cognisance of relevant political factors in three jurisdictions throughout most of the present century; namely the Irish Republic, Northern Ireland and Scotland. Approaches to the language by their respective political authorities have differed considerably over the period.

IRELAND: Until around 1645, Gaelic was the language of the whole island. Significantly, it managed to absorb challenges from Norse and Norman English in their earlier invasions of Ireland in the Dark Ages and Middle Ages respectively. However, with the seventeenth century Anglo-Scottish Plantation of Ulster, and the subsequent English Cromwellian and Williamite re-settlements causing the disintegration of the old Gaelic order, the Irish language became an inevitable victim of enforced anglicisation.

*1 A combination of the anti-Catholic Penal Laws, imposition of an English legal and administrative system, and English domination of the Irish economy and emergent educational system all sufficed to hasten the demise of Gaelic - primarily the language of the Irish peasant - and its replacement by the ascendant English language.

The mid-nineteenth century Irish potato famine also wrecked havoc on the native language, in terms of mass emigration and general de-population of the Gaeltacht areas.

In North East Ulster throughout the eighteenth and nineteenth centuries, there existed a Scots-English language (Lallan) among

Presbyterian descendants of the Lowlands Planters.*2 However, this language was never wholly detached from the mainstream English, and lacking definite roots, ultimately failed to survive as a separate culture or alternative Protestant / Planter identity.

Reliable figures for native Gaelic speakers are difficult to gauge, especially for the pre-census era .However, among the various period surveys undertaken, there is a consistent trend towards anglicisation that accelerated throughout the nineteenth century. According to Wakefield's survey, the mainly monoglot Gaelic-speaking population of Ireland in 1812 was 3,000,000 from a total population of 5,937,856; a figure that by 1812 had increased in line with rapid population growth to 4,100,000 out of a total population of 8,175,124. By contrast, the 1851 Government Census, the first to follow the famine, showed a sharp population decline, with concomitant consequences for the Gaelic language. The total population had been reduced by around 1.7 million to 6,552,356 with registered speakers down to 1,524,286 (23%), of whom only 319,602 were listed as monoglot Gaels.

Evidently, even among native speakers bilingualism had taken hold, which in view of the vast socio-economic advantages accruing to the English medium, left Gaels at a grave disadvantage. Thereafter,the decline in spoken Gaelic accelerated. The 1861 Census put native speakers at 1,105,536 (19.1%) from a total Irish population of 5,798,564; by 1891 these numbers had dropped further to 680,174(14.5%) from an overall population of 4,704,750.

The formation in 1893 of Conradh na Gaelige/The Gaelic Language, under Douglas Hyde and Eoin Mac Neill, was aimed at stemming the language's further decline. However, its principal efforts were directed more towards Gaelic Revivalism among the growing literary population of non-native speakers, than any defence of the dwindling Gaeltachtai. Consequently, native speaking Gaels continued to dwindle; with the 1911 Census putting their numbers at 582,446 (13.3%), from a total - also reducing- all-Ireland population of 4,390,319. Moreover, the great majority of native speakers were concentrated in West coast Gaeltachtai in the counties of Donegal, Mayo, Galway and Kerry, with additional small Gaeltacht communities in rural parts of Cork, Waterford, Louth, Tyrone, Derry, Rathlin Island and the Antrim Glens.

Significantly , with the exception of Galway, no other Gaeltacht covered a large town, and even among Gaeltacht dwellers Gaelic monoglotism had all but disappeared by 1922. Conversely, bilingualism was by then established, which in the long term proved detrimental to the survival of spoken Gaelic within the Gaeltachtai.*3 The Gaelic revivalist efforts were fundamentally impaired by two problems: first, English was the language of economic and social advancement at home; second, English was the essential language of emigration. Both these factors proved crucial in an Ireland whose agrarian economy rendered her subordinate to the economic power of her then British masters.

Yet notwithstanding the failure of its popular revivalist campaign, the Gaelic League affected events at other levels.It became a proselytiser for language and culture to the growing independence movement. As separate studies by A.Hepburn and Tomas O'Fiach showed, reviving the language and Gaelic sports were deemed essential towards fostering a distinctive Gaelic-Irish identity in order to counter-poise the further cultural anglicisation of Ireland.

*4 Gaelic League ideals were adopted by the generation of early Nationalist leaders, whose agenda for an independent Ireland included a high priority for the Irish language, both in defending the remaining Gaeltachtai and also by developing a Gaelic-learning programme through education and the arts for the wider population.

A more populist organisations, on account of its sporting profile was Cumann Luthchleas Gael/Gaelic Athletic Association(GAA), was founded in 1884. This body was motivated by the same cultural nationalism as its Gaelic League brethren; it being dedicated to the revival and popularisation of the ancient Gaelic field sport of hurling, along with devising a specific code for Gaelic football. As is shown by the GAA records, its early growth was assisted by a natural sporting appeal to nationalist youth, as well as Catholic clerical backing; the Catholic archbishops of Cashel and Tuam, Croke and Mc Hale, being among early Association patrons.

*5 Indeed Croke's acceptance letter to Michael Cusack highlighted his sentiments about defending the Gaelic heritage against the encroaching forces of anglicisation:

*"One of the most painful...and..frequently recurring reflections that, as an Irishman, I am compelled to make..is derived from the ugly fact that we are daily importing from England, not only her manufactured goods, which we cannot help doing,since she has practically strangled our own manufacturing appliances, but, together with her fashions, her accents, her vicious literature, her music, her dances and her manifold mannerisms, her games also, and her pastimes , to the utter discredit of our own grand national sports, and to the sore humiliation, as I believe, of every genuine son and daughter of the old land".*6 (See Appendix 1 for the full text of this letter)

Such was the GAA's rapid growth that within thirty five years virtually every nationalist district in Ireland boasted its own Gaelic sports club.This link between cultural and political nationalism proved effective,both for publications and manpower. Additionally, the alliance between Gaelic linguists and Gaelic sportsmen in common pursuit of an independent, Christian Ireland had a moral character that has scarcely been acknowledged by historians,but was important in its appeal to the Catholic clergy .Its essence was highlighted in a letter from the Down GAA secretary,published in local newspaper in 1910:

"Go through any popular district of County Down on a Sunday and see the number of young men loitering in the precinct of the public house: see their careless and slovenly gait. Go into the hurling or football (Gaelic)field, and see their agile figures and elastic step. Which of these bodies will be more effective in regenerating Ireland? It will not be the Sunday loafer whose thoughts cannot get outside the confines of the "Bung". I look upon the young men of Down - Newry in particular - to support the pastimes of

*the Gael: by doing so thy are working concomitantly with the Gaelic League, the political and industrial movement for a regenerated Ireland".*7*

Such sentiments were not lost on an Irish clergy who saw in the Gaelic movement an opportunity for proper exercise of pastoral influence. This was to become an indelible characteristic of the GAA over the ensuing eighty years,thereby giving it something of a clerical identity that was politically restrictive.

It is significant that the Gaelic generation figured several leading nationalists whose prominence in the separatist movement 1912 - 22, and leadership of the infant Irish Free State (whether as Free Staters or Republicans) after 1922 lent high status to the Gaelic language and culture. They included the Gaeilgeoir educationalist, poet and executed 1916 Rising leader, Padraig Pearse; Antrim-bred former British Civil Servant,humanitarian and nationalist convert, Sir Roger Casement, himself executed by HMG in 1916; another Antrim native, historian and Volunteers organiser, Professor Eoin Mac Neill, who became education minister in the first Free State government; and Sinn Fein Leader 1917-22 Fianna Fail founder (1925) and Taoiseach/President thereafter, Eamon De Valera. To this school, nationalism meant more than political self-determination; it embraced Ireland's Gaelic heritage,with promotion by future Irish governments.

It's ethos had been summarised by Eoin Mac Neill's appeal to the Irish clergy in Ecclesiastical Review as early as 1891.

"We Irish have resisted fusion for seven centuries, with the result that we are still a living, energetic and self-reliant nation,and as capable of doing a nation's work as on the first day that Strongbow first landed in Ireland. Fusion was prevented first by the difference of language and physical resistance; afterwards by difference of language and religion; latterly by religion alone. Were this last difference removed, as it yet may be, most probably by our own influence, it is a mere illusion to hope that national character could, without some other defence, withstand the forces of assimilation. Politics will not form a defence, for politics is not to be dreamt of.Clearly, unless the national character remains to attract the national

aspirations and leaven the national life, Ireland must become a mere geographical expression. *8

The synthesis of political and cultural nationalism, so eloquently presented by Mac Neill, proved to be the guiding ethos for the entire separatist movement, and figured prominently in its agenda for an independent Ireland. Padraig Pearse, writing in The United Irishman in 1905, put the case even more succinctly:

"The Irish language is an essential of Irish nationality.I t is more, it is chief depository and safeguard. When the Irish language disappears, Irish nationality will ipso facto disappear, and for ever. Political autonomy can be lost and recovered, and lost again and recovered again....Now if Ireland were to lose her language - which is, remember, an essential of her nationality - there might conceivably be a free state in Ireland at some future date: but that state would not be the Irish nation, for it would have parted from the body of traditions which constitute Irish nationality".

Accordingly, in the years following independence, Gaeilgeoiri policies constituted the first real consensus between the Free State party (that subsequently became Fine Gael) of W.T.Cosgrave and Eamon De Valera's pro-republican Fianna Fail.*9 This "consensus" also included the Catholic Church, who as Hindley and O'Cuiv - from their different positions - each acknowledge, had long proved to be a reliable sponsor of Gaelic interests in education and culture.*10

Policies adopted included a compulsory language learning programme at all levels of education, with basic Gaelic being required for school leavers, university entrants and public servants.There was also a bilingual public communications policy for official documents and notices, broadcasting and statutory bodies, which required Gaelic usage at least as an option. Significantly,a comprehensive programme of assistance to the Gaeltachtai followed by way of grants, provision of native-speaking school teachers, a Gaeltacht radio station (founded in 1972), and the creation of a Gaeltacht ministry in 1956 to encourage economic investment in order to halt de-population. Most recently, in 1996, came the launching of Teilifis na Gaelige, an all-Irish medium television channel. Additionally, the Irish state has consistently provided special assistance to the increasing range of Gaelic sports and cultural organisations. Beneficiaries have included Conradh na Gaelige, Gaelinn (a separate Gaeilgeoiri group), Glor na nGael in Northern Ireland, and the Gaelic Athletic Association plus others, all of whom are actively promoting Gaelic culturalism in their respective fields.

Gaelic promotion has rendered mixed results.The same socio-economic pressures from the years of British rule continued to undermine the Gaeltacht communities for long after 1922, causing their numbers to decline further. Indeed the twin factors of emigration and ever-increasing travel/tele-communications diminished the cultural isolation on which the Gaeltacht depended, thereby making their survival prospects look bleak. Bilingualism also undermined the native-speaking character of the Gaeltachtai. The 1971 and 1981 Censuses put Gaelic speakers in the Republic at 789,429 (28.3%) and 1,018,413 (31,6%) respectively. Native-speaking numbers are difficult to estimate accurately, but these could not exceed 60,000. Inevitably survival will depend on a mixture of continuing government aid, economic regeneration, an effective educational programme and a general climate of positive thinking within and beyond the Gaeltachtai.

On the positive side, there has been a substantial Gaelic cultural regeneration at all levels, which has left a particular mark on rural Irish life. Although Gaeltachtai dwellers have declined, the level of Gaelic literacy among the wider population has increased to a figure exceeding 1.1 million. Significantly, there is an established and popular Gaelic cultural scene in arts,Gaelic sports,music and literature. The recent launching of Teilifis na Gaelige builds on the experience of Radio na Gaeltachta. While the obligatory Gaelic-learning programme has not been universally popular with sections of leftist and non-nationalist opinion, nevertheless it is difficult to imagine how Ireland's Gaelic ethos could survive without its prominence in the school curriculum. Moreover, additional to the Irish state and Gaelic League with its sister organisations, elsewhere the Gaelic ethos has been most effectively promoted by two broadly complimentary nationalist associations, Fianna Fail and the Gaelic Athletic Association. Both have large rank and file memberships, with deep roots in rural and small urban communities, which in the GAA case extends to the nationalist community of Northern Ireland Also, both apply the Gaelic language,symbols and cultural priorities to an extent that enables them to claim the high ground of Irish patriotism.

Ulster Factor: It is significant that among the four provinces of Ireland, until the seventeenth century Plantation, Ulster was the most Gaelicised of all. This fact is generally agreed among leading historians like A.T.Q Stewart and P.O'Snodaigh.*11 There the language prevailed, as did the Gaelic order, inclusive of the clans, chieftains and Brehon laws .Equally significant was the province's historic link with Scotland, from where North-East Ulster (specifically the modern counties of Antrim and Down) was separated by only a short sea-way, and with whom there had long been close cultural, ethnic and commercial links, underpinned by centuries of cross-migration.

The Plantation changed all that, with the introduction of an Anglo-Scottish Ascendancy of mixed Presbyterian and Anglican religious character. Also, there was an imposed English legal system, and significantly, the enforced anglicisation of language and cultural environment. Those changes had far-reaching effects on the emergent socio-political culture of the province, which over the ensuing centuries acquired a distinctive Scots/Irish character that caused it to resemble the Lowlands of Scotland more than anything recognisably Irish. Such characteristics were of great consequence to the evolution of rival Unionist and Nationalist forces in twentieth century Ulster, as too was the politically beleaguered position of the Gaelic language.

The process of linguistic anglicisation occurred at a varying pace, for which different perspectives are held by the various academic authorities. A.T.Q Stewart in his account of the evolution of modern Ulster, acknowledges the place of spoken Gaelic among the native Irish, but notes its gradual demise throughout the late eighteenth and nineteenth centuries under the pressures of semi-industrialisation and lingering repressive legislation against the native Irish peasantry.*12 There was also the economic and political dominance of the Anglo-Scottish planter population, whose numbers were heavily concentrated in the north-eastern counties of Down and Antrim, but extended to the fertile plains of mid-Ulster, east Tyrone, Derry and Armagh. Although predominantly Presbyterian by the early eighteenth century, with the majority speaking a dialect of Scots-English (Lallan), in fact until the 1820's Scottish Gaelic also held a strong following among the rural Presbyterian communities along the east Ulster coast. Maolcholaim Scott noted a tendency among eighteenth century Presbyterian ministers in the south Ulster counties of Armagh and Monaghan to preach in the Gaelic tongue, culminating in 1719 in the publication of a Gaelic (Irish) Presbyterian catechism.*13 Among the native Irish Catholic) population access to any form of religious literature or education in the eighteenth century was difficult, owing to the repressive Penal Laws. Additionally, there was then the Catholic practice of publishing Church literature in Latin, which proved unhelpful for matching the medium of its Gaelic-speaking followers. However, in so far as Catholic priests could operate in the repressive Penal climate of seventeenth and eighteenth century Ulster, they did so, using the Gaelic language for conducting their ministry. In that respect, the fugitive clergymen provided effectively the only educated Gaelic leadership for guiding their dispossessed brethren through an era of cultural mutation. Accordingly, such few Gaelic publications as did appear were noteworthy on account of their rarity. Of the latter, Seamus MacGiolla Fhinnein's scholarly study of the seventeenth Down 'Hedge School' master, Eoin O'Ghripin, who translated the Catholic catechism from Latin into

Gaelic,provides a valuable insight to a scarce breed of Ulster Gaelic scribes from the Penal period.*14

Elsewhere, among the enduring Ulster Gaeltachtai, both numbers and communities dwindled throughout the course of the nineteenth and early twentieth centuries.According to Seamus O'Casaide's authoritative study, spoken Gaelic disappeared from Down before the onset of the Great War.*15 Thereafter, the minor Gaeltachtai of Tyrone, the Sperrins (Derry), Antrim Glens and Rathlin Island followed suit by the 1940s, leaving Donegal as the sole county with active Gaeltacht communities in present times.

What is significant about the Ulster experience is that at different times since the mid-seventeenth century the Gaelic language has been subject to cross-communal influences. While predominantly rooted in the Irish nationalist tradition, nevertheless there was also an accommodation of Plantation Scottish culture, complete with its Scottish-Gaelic antecedents. The latter preceded the 1798 Presbyterian-led United Irishmen's insurrection of Ulster, but throughout the nineteenth century there followed the socio-economic and ultimate political assimilation of Ulster Presbyterians into the vanguard of Irish unionism. Thereafter, Presbyterian culture alignments reflected the anglophile, non-Celtic course so beloved of the Unionist political establishment. Moreover, the increasing link between Gaeilgeoir lobbyists in the Gaelic League and Gaelic Athletic Association respectively and Nationalist politics increased Unionist antipathy towards both language and culture .By the time of partition in 1921, Gaelicism was viewed by Unionists as an appendix to Sinn Feinism, and thus there existed no desire for either supporting the language or its cultural ancillaries in the new Northern state. Hence it was inevitable that faced with consistent political hostility from the Stormont administration, Gaelic interests became linked to the politics and culture of Northern Ireland's Nationalist community.

Scotland: The historical experience of Scottish Gaeldom has much in common with that of their Irish brethren but diverged with the distinctive course of Scottish history.

Unlike Ireland, where the Gaelic language is central to the national cultural heritage, conversely Gaelic was never the exclusive tongue of all Scots, though until the Middle Ages it was the language of a great majority of Scotland's population. Moreover, save for a period in the early Middle Ages, Gaelic has not commanded principal place in Scotland's modern political or institutional development, nor its cultural evolution. The Gaelic order went unrecognised in modern Scots law and civil administration, even ahead of the enforced Anglo-Scottish Union of 1707. Thereafter it disintegrated under Crown repression.

It is not that Gaelic is either alien or peripheral to the Scottish heritage, but its contemporary legacy is concentrated in the Highlands, Hebrides and West Coast. Therefore it is accurate to speak of Gaelic as "an" rather than "the" historic language of Scotland. Significantly, Scots were forced to co-habit alongside other races; the dominant of which were Welsh-speaking North Britons in the central valley and Southern Scotland, Picts in the eastern areas north of the Firth of Forth, and Northumbrian Angles extending south from the Lothians. Additionally, there were the Norse influences that embraced the Orkneys, Shetlands and northern Highlands. All have left a mark on contemporary Scottish society, but in so far as the others have all been absorbed into a Lowlands culture, as highlighted by Withers' study, Gaeldom has proved the most enduring and also the most resilient to historical anglicisation. *16

As regards the introduction of Gaelic to Scotland, this subject has divided historians. However, substantial evidence points to a migration of Gaelic-speaking Scots from their historic clan lands in the north- east of Ireland to the western Scottish Highlands- specifically modern Argyll - around the first century AD. This migration followed on from existing Ulster/Scottish links, based on both sides of the narrow Sea of Moyle, such as the ancient Gaelic kingdom of Dalriada, covering large parts of North Antrim and

Western Argyll. Indeed, according to the great Celtic saga, Ruraiocht, the exploits of Ulster's famed Gaelic warriors, including the legendary Cuchullian - "hound and defender of Ulster" - from Emain Macha (Armagh), abound with references to crossing the sea to the brethren in Alba (Scotland). Later, the sixth century evangelisation of the Scots was undertaken by the Northern Irish monk, Columdcille (Columba), who established a Celtic church across the whole country. The subsequent triumph of the Gaelic language and customs, and conquest of the Picts, was completed under the fist recognised King of Scots and Picts, Kenneth MacAlpin, in 844 AD.

Thereafter, Gaelic assumed an expanding influence into the southern Lowlands and modern Border territories, which continued up to the eleventh century, until the reign of Malcolm Canmore and his English wife, the saintly Margaret Mary. Gaelic was not rapidly displaced, so much as slowly supplanted at the Court with first, Norman French, and then English. As Kenneth MacKinnon and Withers in their respective studies have each recognised, a combination of military and commercial influences, plus shifting political authority in medieval Scotland, caused the gradual Anglicisation of the southern Lowlands, which was to prevail over most of Scotland, except the Highlands, within the next three centuries.*17 At the same time, as the Gaelic historian, John Bannerman, acknowledges,among the ordinary population Gaelic experienced a slow demise, and was still widely spoken, even among Lowland Scots at the time of Knox's early sixteenth century Presbyterian Reformation.*18

Identifying the Gaelic decline in post-Reformation Scotland is a complex area, and one expertly covered by Bannerman and Withers in their respective historical treaties. For the purpose of this book, it is enough to say that by the time of the Act of Union (1707) with england, Scotland's Gaels were confined to the Highlands,Hebrides and Galloway in the south-west. Elsewhere, as the late Glasgow University historian, George Pryde, observed, Scotland had developed a commercial culture and accompanying political order based on mercantilist trade, along with Presbyterian social ethics in such areas as education and legal practice,and, increasingly, Crown patronage.*19 Significantly, Scots-English had replaced Gaelic as the principal language of both the anglophile Edinburgh establishment and ordinary Lowlanders. None of these factors bode well for the Gaelic language, nor did subsequent trends towards urbanisation, industrialisation and political democratisation.

An additional problem for Gaeldom was the low status of the language in the Lowlands from the early eighteenth century onwards. This was reflected in the marked preference among several Highlands clan chieftains for adopting English and Edinburgh Scots-English culture in place of indigenous Gaelic; a practice that percolated to kinsmen with depressing effects. Pryde also noted the tendency of migrating Highlanders to conceal their Gaelic roots by adopting anglicised names and speech forms.*20 Such were the hostile political atmosphere in the Lowlands following the Jacobite insurrection of 1745/46.

The legacy of that Jacobite defeat at Culloden (April 1746) proved devastating for the Highland clans generally, and Gaelic language particularly. Pryde, Withers and Bannerman in their respective accounts tell how the Gaelic order was swept away in the climate of intensive Crown-sponsored hostility aimed at all sections of Highland Gaeldom, which was held synonymous with Jacobinism. The 1746 Disarming Act prohibited Highland dress (kilts) and pipes, and though not specifically barring the Gaelic language, nevertheless it was targeted at the Gaelic clans, who had lately supported Charles Edward Stuart (Bonnie Prince Charlie) and previously resisted the political authority of both the Crown and Edinburgh administration. Although that repressive statute was repealed in 1782, by then de-Gaelicisation was well under way in the Highlands.

In that sense, its purpose was similar to Crown policies in Ireland, notably cultural anglicisation, as a corollary of political submission.

Other related causes of decline included the Highland clearances, itself a notorious practice of eighteenth and nineteenth century Highland landlords, who forced tenant crofters off their holdings to make way for the more profitable infusion of sheep.This repressive saga caused the enforced depopulation of the Highlands and Islands to the order of over 400,000 crofters and cotters; and, as with the Irish potato famine, remains embedded in contemporary popular culture as a grievous injustice perpetrated by Crown-sponsored landlords against ordinary crofting Gaels.The clearances produced a mass migration towards the urban centres of Glasgow, Edinburgh, Dundee and the cities of England. Like the Irish potato famine, the clearances also produced a mass of emigrants towards the colonies of Australia, New Zealand and Canada; with the latter attracting substantial numbers of displaced Gaelic-speaking crofters and cotters, as is evidenced by the strong Gaelic traditions of latter day Nova Scotia and Cape Breton Island (Canada).

External factors aside, there was also the nature of Scotland's emerging educational system - arguably Europe's most advanced - which followed the Calvinist principal of educating all to read the Scriptures. This meant extending literacy to every Scottish village, without penalising the poor .However, this code of Presbyterian egalitarianism did not extend to a purposeful defence of the Gaelic language, far less the incorporation of Gaelic into the school medium. Conversely, the dominant attitudes of the nineteenth century Anglo-Scottish Unionist establishment linked Gaelic to Jacobite ideals, which were politically threatening. Additionally, there was the low educational status of Gaelic, which was decried in Edinburgh's urbane circles as a backward language of the non-advanced Highlands and Islands and Ireland, and best assisted by a mixture of economic and educational developments to a peaceful demise. Indeed as MacKinnon recounts, the use of education and schools to rid Scotland of what one inspector contemptuously referred to as "..the Gaelic nuisance..." was both blatant and Crown-sponsored. Those overt prejudices were reflected in the Educational

Act (Scotland)1872, which MacKinnon noted:

"...was passed without recognition that the Highlands were an area of particular linguistic significance within a national educational system. No specific references to Gaelic were contained within the Act." *21

The Act created school boards in each parish and burgh, and to those bodies were transferred all schools created under Parliamentary authority by an earlier act of 1838. These included charitable schools run by various Presbyterian groups and societies, specifically The Society in Scotland for the Propagation of Christian Knowledge (SSPCK), General Assembly of the church of Scotland, Free Church of Scotland, and the Gaelic Schools Societies. Previously the Free Church (formed after the Disruption in the General Assembly of the Church of Scotland,1843) with its Highlands and Islands base, and SSPCK had actively proselytised in the vernacular Gaelic tongue, thereby ensuring for it a regular medium of usage. Indeed the Free Church Kirk, along with the Gaelic Bible translation and special metric Psalms, provided a valuable kernel for Gaelic speakers and preachers, which was used in the education of Highlands and Hebridean children throughout the nineteenth century. However the 1872 Act swept away even the peripheral place of Gaelic in the Highlands educational structure. Under the new regime, Gaelic was actively discouraged in schools, while the appointment of English-speaking teachers was common, even in monoglot Gaidhealtacht districts. Indeed so vindictive was the de-Gaelicisation education policy that a further corollary of the 1872 Act was the unsavoury practice of whipping native-speaking children with the 'maide-crocaidh', a stick on a cord, as punishment for communicating in their native tongue on school premises. As noted by MacKinnon, the law of the 'maide-cochaidh' was continued on the Isle of Lewis - Scotland's largest Gaidhealtachd - up until the 1930s. It is significant that those punitive anti-Gaelic measures prevailed until well into the current century. Not until 1918 was any Scottish educational reform initiated that gave positive recognition to the role of Gaelic in schools, either as a subject or medium for learning. Moreover, the attainment of even modest concessions was due in no small way to the lobbyist activities of groups like An Comunn Gaidhealach - founded in 1891, and which emerged as Scotland's equivalent of Conradh na Gaelige - and the Gaelic Society of London. Both those organisations provided an influential voice for Scottish Gaeldom throughout lean times, which both concentrating on education and the cultural domain rather than political front, as with Ireland.

In terms of numbers, like Ireland, Scotland's Gaelic-speaking population was not easy to quantify in the last century. This was partly due to the reluctance of many native Gaelic speakers to admit their normal medium to the Census enumerators, for reasons previously discussed. There was also a difficulty about identifying monoglot Gaelic speakers in the Highlands and Hebrides, as distinct from bilingual Gaels both there and all over Scotland. Furthermore, only after 1881 did the official Census seek information about Gaelic-speaking practices among the Scottish population over three years of age. In 1881, 231,594 persons claimed to first medium Gaelic speakers , out of a total Scottish population of 3,425,151. By 1951, Gaelic speakers had declined to 95,447 (out of 4,826,814) and by 1961 to 80,978 (out of 4,892,882).*22 Predictably, the Gaidhealtacht in the 1880s included large parts of Arran, Bute, parts of Sutherland, Ross-shire and Inverness-shire, Skye and the islands of the Inner Hebrides, along with Lewis, Harris, Barra, the Uists and the other islands of the Outer Hebrides. However, by the 1950s the mainland Gaidhealtachd had contracted to a few small communities in the Western Highlands, with only reasonable-sized Gaidhealtachd being found in Skye, Lewis, Harris and the smaller islands of the Outer Hebrides. Significantly, this Hebridean Gaidhealtachd was to prove a crucial factor in the subsequent creation of a Gaelic local authority, Comhairle nan Eilean (Western Isles Council), in the mid-1970s.

It is noteworthy that during the last three decades of the nineteenth century there emersed an assertiveness on the part of

Gaels and crofters.Resistance to evictions, formation of the Highland Land League, agitation against tyrannical landlordism, crofter reform campaigns and the launching of the Gaelic lobbyist organisations....all testified to a growing self-confidence that was sweeping Highlands popular culture at that time. Significantly, there was encouragement from sister organisation in Ireland like Conradh na Gaelige, Cumann Luthchleas Gael and the Irish Land League. However, Pryde's account of the period indicates that Highlands groups were less politically potent than their Irish counterparts.*23 This was partly due to the regional appeal of Gaelic culture in Scotland, and partly because Scottish Gaels sought only a positive recognition of their language and culture, whereas for Irish Gaels the language and cultural revival augmented a wider goal of political nationhood.

It is noteworthy that despite a nascent interest in Scottish home rule from the 1880s onwards, early Scottish nationalists did not give prominent sponsorship to the Gaelic language cause, along Irish lines. Indeed Scotland's early home rulers tended to be liberal, with the addition of some socialists. However, both parties were essentially United Kingdom constitutional reformers. As for the Scottish nationalist movement, as Jack Brand recounts, it was slow in reaching birth and muted in its programme.*24 There was a disinclination among the latter's pioneers to embrace Gaelicism, as it appeared marginal to mainstream Scottish society in Glasgow,Edinburgh and Dundee; thus a close identification it was feared might limit the nationalist appeal.

Interestingly, over the first quarter of the twentieth century, as a result of the lobbyist activities of groups like An Comunn Gaidhealach and the London Gaelic Society, there had been an easing of erstwhile anti-Gaelic prejudices by various wings of the Scottish educational and political establishment. In 1915 there was the introduction of a public secondary schools examination in Gaelic. Following on from the lobbying of An Comunn Gaidhealach, the 1918 Education (Scotland) Act included a mandatory Gaelic clause, which though proving ineffective as far as initiating Gaelic-medium education went, nevertheless marked a beginning of the slow Gaelic incorporation to Scottish education. Even the Gaelic Mods and Feisain (cultural festivals of Gaelic music,drama and arts), organised by A.C.G., came to enjoy a rising esteem far and beyond the Highlands and Hebrides.

From those green shoots, other developments - covered in later chapters - followed over ensuing decades. However, it is enough to say that by the end of World War 1, surviving servicemen returning to the Highlands and Islands found an area seething with discontent. The region was rapidly de-populating, as tens of thousands left in search of employment in Glasgow, Edinburgh,England and Canada. There was popular agitation by crofters in pursuit of land rights, and various other campaigns waged by fishermen, ex-servicemen and tenant workers. Given Gaelic's dependence on a Highlands/Hebridean social infra-structure, it seemed likely that with the latter in serious decline, the language had poor prospects. Thus the twentieth century for Scottish Gaeldom, like its Irish counterparts, has figured a battle for its very survival.

FOOTNOTES / REFERENCES

1. See D. Figgis *The Gaelic State in the Past and Future (Dublin, 1917)*
K.Nicholls *Gaelic and Gaelicised Ireland in the Middle Ages (Dublin 1972)*
R.F Foster *Modern Ireland (London,1988).*

2. See P.S Robinson *The Scots Language in Seventeenth century Ulster; Ulster Folklife, Vol.35,1989, pp.86-99.* Michael Montgomery
The Anglicisation of Scots in Seventeenth century Ulster; Studies in Scottish Literature; Vol. 266,1991, pp 50-64. John Hewitt *Rhyming weavers and other country poets of Antrim and Down (Belfast, 1974)* Mairi Robinson (ed.) *The Concise Scots Dictionary (Aberdeen,1985)*

3. Reg Hindley*Death of the Irish Language: A qualified obituary (London, 1990)*

4. A.C Hepburn *The Conflict of Nationality in Modern Ireland (London, 1990)* Tomas O'Fiaich *The Language and Political History; in A View of the Irish Language,Ed B.O'Cuiv (Dublin,1969)*

5. See *Treorai Oifigiuil/Official Guide, 1992 - Gaelic Athletic Association/Cumann Luthchleas Gael - pp 92/93.*

6. Treorai Oifigiuil, 1992, p.92

7. Letter to Frontier Sentinel, 1st October,1910, from Charles Magee, Down GAA secretary. - Cited in O Shiol go Blath/The Down GAA History, 1884-1990: - Sighle Nic An Ultaigh (Newry,1990).

8.Eoin MacNeill *An Appeal to the Clergy of Ireland; cited in: Brian O'Cuiv The Gaelic Cultural Movement and the New Nationalism; and Kevin B. Nowlan (ed). The Making of 1916: Studies in the History of the Rising (Dublin,1969).*

9. Hindley (1990), Chap 3.

10. See *Hindley, Chaps.3 &10; O'Cuiv (ed).1969.*

11. A.T.Q Stewart *The Narrow Ground:Aspects of Ulster,1609 - 1969 (London, 1977)* P.O'Snodaigh *Hidden Ulster (Belfast 1973).*

12 Stewart, 1977.

13. Maolchalaim Scott *When Planter was the Gael; Fortnight supplement (Belfast, 1993)*

14. *Seamus MacGiolla Fhinnein (Ang. J.B Mac Aleenan) Teagasc Criostai Ui Ghripin'; M.A thesis,University of Ulster,Coleraine,1990.*

15. Seamus O'Casaide *The Irish Language in Belfast and Ciunty Down (Dublin,1930).*

16. C.W.J Withers *Gaelic in Scotland 1698-1981: The Geographical History of a Language (Edinburgh,1984)*

17. See *Withers (1984) chaps.1-3.* Kenneth MacKinnon *Gaelic: A Past and Future Prospect; chaps. 2-3 (Edinburgh,1991)*

18. John Bannerman *Studies in the History of Dalriada (Edinburgh,1974)*

19. George Pryde *Scotland from 1603 to the Present Day: A New History of Scotland; Vol.2, chaps,xii &xiii, (Edinburgh, 1962).*

20. *Pryde (1962), chap,xiv.*

21 *MacKinnon (1991), p.74.*

22. *Ibid, p.90.*

23. *Pryde (1962), chaps, xxiii -xxv.*

24. Jack Brand *The National Movement in Scotland (London,1978) chaps,11-13.*

CHAPTER 2
1920 - 1965: GAELDOM'S BARREN YEARS.

The years 1920-1965 represented the nadir of Gaeldom's fortunes in Scotland and Northern Ireland. Over that period, the steady decline in native speakers in both countries was accentuated by a failure to make substantial headway in any of the vital social areas; namely education, publishing, the arts and broadcasting.Only a changing social climate by the early 1960s, along with assiduous lobbying in Scotland, made changes feasible.

Scotland experienced a substantial drop in the numbers of Gaelic speakers, plus a declining Gaidhealtachd .Although minor openings occurred in education, arts and the media towards the end of the 1950s, nevertheless Scottish Gaels appeared to be an increasingly marginalised community, restricted to the West Highlands and Hebrides. Conversely, Ulster Gaeldom was forced into a political ghetto over this period, caused by the hostility of successive Unionist administrations at Belfast, headed by Craigavon, Andrews and Brookeborough respectively. The ethos of the Northern state was explicitly Unionist and anti-Irish. By contrast, Ulster Gaeilgeoirism and the Gaelic League were linked to Nationalist opposition to the state. Accordingly, the Gaelic language and culture were denied recognition, and thus effectively forced into an alliance with Nationalism in consequence. Additionally, native-speaking Gaels finally became extinct in the Six Counties by the late 1940s, leaving Donegal (and Omeath until 1983) as the surviving Ulster Gaeltacht communities in contemporary times.

SOUTHERN IRELAND: Interestingly, despite the lean times experienced by Ulster and Scottish Gaels throughout those decades, the Gaeilgeoir orthodoxy of the infant Southern state was well advanced. Irish language teaching had been made compulsory in all schools, and Irish was later introduced as a mandatory subject in the Leaving Certificate examinations, as well as being made a requirement for university, broadcasting and public sector entry. University College, Galway, went further in adopting a strict Gaelic fluency requirement for all undergraduates entrants, while also scheduling many lectures/seminars in the native tongue. So too had the languages primacy been effectively asserted by the Constitution. Additionally, the range of Gaelic language organisations like Conradh na Gaelige, Gael Linn, Cumann Luthchleas Gael, Comhaltas Ceolteori na hEireann (traditional music association)and others became eligible for generous funding from the Irish state.Successive Dublin governments also attempted to stem the economic decline and depopulation of the Gaeltachtai by a mixture of socio-economic intervention, provision of educational facilities and payment of a small annual grant - the Deontas- to all native Gaelic speakers. There was also the creation of a Gaeltacht ministry in 1956, with the aim of encouraging investment in the Gaeltachtai, and thus halting de-population. The introduction of Radio na Gaeltacht 1972 was intended as a further step in that direction. Whether this programme actually enhanced the language in the long term, or supplemented a growing interest lobby within the civic structures, is a matter of ongoing debate?

That issue shall be addressed later in this book.

As regards the surviving Gaeltachtai, numbers of first language Gaels are hard to quantify, given the penchant for grouping native speakers together with second language Gaels. The 1926 Census (covering only the Twenty Six Counties) put the number of Irish-speakers at 540,000(19.3% of the population) a figure that had increased to 716,420 (27.2%) by the time of the 1961 Census, 789,429 (28.3%0 by 1971 and 1,018,413 (31.6%) by 1981. However, reliable estimates tally on the conclusion that native speakers could not have much exceeded 75,000 by 1981.

The degree to which Government neglect and/or the effects of anglicisation accelerated the Gaeltachtai decline is hotly debated between academics and Gaeilgeoiri. What is clear is that the independent Irish Free State facilitated the Gaelic language and culture to a degree far surpassing Scotland and Northern Ireland. In the circumstances, a searching examination of Gaeldom, past and present in both countries, is necessary.

SCOTLAND The decline of Scottish Gaeldom in the years 1920-65 had become apparent on several fronts.

First, there was the continuing decline in the numbers of native Gaelic speakers, which put at risk the future of the Hebridean Gaidhealtachd. Census figures showed native-speaking numbers to have dropped from 136,135 to 95,447 in the period 1931 to 1951, and again to 80,620 by 1961. *1 Causes were self evident. A weakened Hebridean economy, along with the depressed state of crofting and fisheries, ensured a population haemorage abroad and to the Mainland.*23 Similar conditions prevailed in the surviving Gaidhealtachtd pockets of the West Highlands over the same period, with the result that by 1960 native speakers had disappeared from all but a few villages in the West Highlands.

The effects were to prove devastating to the interests of the Gaelic language in Scotland. A contracting Gaidhealtachd meant poor morale among remaining dwellers, declining socio-economic infrastructure in the Highlands and Hebrides, reduced educational need, population imbalance and a generally uncertain future for Scottish Gaeldom. The latter was especially applicable, given the increasing pressures for anglicisation in the business and educational worlds as the century progressed.

In Scottish education, despite the modest openings acquired through the 1918 Education (Scotland) Act, with its mandatory Gaelic clause, still Gaelic remained a marginal subject everywhere. It went untaught in most Scottish schools until the late 1950s, and was even downgraded in the Highlands and Islands, where the Gaidhealtachd might have justified a more inclusive policy.Significantly, there was an absence of Gaelic medium education in all areas, including the Hebridean Gaidhealtachd; a factor that did little to raise the status of Gaelic among native speakers and the wider population alike.

Gaelic publishing and written works were scarce to the point of being non-existent in those years. Until the creation of a publicly-aided Gaelic publishing house in the 1960s, almost the only new books emerging were Presbyterian catechetical tracts and occasional academic texts. There were virtually no popular books of any kind appearing, nor did a Gaelic language newspaper exist to cater for the Gaidhealtachd communities. By the early 1950s so poor was the provision of literature and low its educational recognition, that Scottish Gaeldom appeared set for a slow but undignified demise, caused by indifference and neglect.

Nor was there any Gaelic arts dimension, far less public assistance for Gaelic drama or musical projects. Only the Mods organised by An Comunn Gaidhealach, provided a mirror of Gaelic cultural life to the wider population. The National Mod, taking place in October at shifting venues around Glasgow, Edinburgh, the Highlands and Hebrides, offered a Gaelic cultural showpiece, that rose in stature with the acquisition of royal patronage from the 1960s onwards. In time, that event came to attract public funding and television coverage to the point where it now numbers among the major events in Scotland's cultural calendar. However, such elevated status was some way off in the negative climate of the 1940s and '50s, and many developments were needed over the ensuing period when the foundations stones were laid.

In stark contrast to Ulster Gaeldom, and indeed that of the rest of Ireland, Scottish Gaeldom was separate from Scottish nationalism. As the political scientist, Jack Brand, observed, because Scottish Gaels were more marginal in numbers and community scope than their Irish counterparts, nationalists thus kept a distance,*3 Nationalists were reluctant to risk alienating urban voters in the Lowlands towns and cities - on whom the then-struggling Scottish National Party depend - by embracing the peripheral Highlands image that Gaeldom exuded.Although the early SNP leadership of

Roland Muir and John MacCormick made positive noises about protecting Gaelic interests, in fact their concept of national identity transcended regional character in favour of a sense of modern Scottish nationhood, where Gaelic would have only a marginal place.*4 Some nationalists were even hostile to any association with Gaeldom. Among them was the literary Scottish socialist-republican, Hugh MacDiarmid, who saw more merit in a Scots (Lallan) rather than Gaelic revival.*5 MacDiarmid argued that because Lallan had a large popular base, rooted in the national heritage, it should be adopted as an alternative medium of literature and symbol of nationhood.

James Hunter's authoritative history of the Highlands and Hebridean crofters links the latter's' struggles to those of Scottish Gaeldom in the late nineteenth and early twentieth centuries.*6 The Gaelic language was common place in those areas where crofting prevailed; hence its character was defined by Highlands Land League campaigns for social justice. Significantly, this legacy endured for the ensuing hundred years, and remains an indelible feature of the folk culture of contemporary Gaeldom.

The only nationalist movement to embrace Gaelic revivalism as a priority was the short-lived 1920s Scots National League. That movement was never large, being confined to less than 1,000 members in a few branches around Glasgow, Edinburgh, London, Liverpool, Dalkieth, Dunfermline and Hamilton.Brand observed:

"..the Scots National League (SNL) was descended from, if it did not embody, the traditions of Gaelic cultural independence movements.It was clear that a great deal of the inspiration was Irish." *8

Hunter's comparison of the struggles of the Irish and Scottish Highland Land Leagues in the late nineteenth and early twentieth centuries, both operating in agrarian economics and oppressed by similarly exploitive landlords, bears serious consideration.

Independence through social and cultural emancipation, inclusive of a revival of the Gaelic identity, had in the 1880s aroused the interest of John Murdoch, a Scot who had worked in Ireland in the

1850s and 60s, but retired to Scotland to edit The Highlander from Inverness. Under Murdoch's editorship, the paper actively propagated the twin causes of land reform and Gaelic revivalism, both of which were familiar themes in Ireland. It is significant that as Irish separatism of that period was spawned by the Gaelic League and Gaelic Athletic Association, so did Murdoch advocate self-government for a re-Gaelicised Scotland. Later the emergent Highland Land League - which managed to get MPs elected from Highlands constituencies - pursued a staunchly pro-Home Rule policy. This factor led Brand to further observe:

"The cultural awakening of the Highlands was to be the basis of a national awakening for Scotland. ...It was from this background that the link emerged between the Gaelic cultural movement and the demand for self-government." *9

Two major figures dominated the SNL. One was a writer, Ruaraidh Erskine of Marr, second son of Lord Erskine, whose two passions were Catholic evangelism and Gaelic revivalism; and the other being playright and businessman, William Gillies.

Erskine founded a number of journals targeted at the Gaelic-speaking or Gaelic-sympathising intelligentsia. Most prominent of his initiatives was Guth na Bliadhna ('Voice of the Year'), which was published partly in Gaelic and partly in English, and ran from 1904 until 19220.*10 His editorials evoked positive images of Gaelic history, institutions and folk culture, while also propagating a distinctive anti-imperial message. Typical of his line was the following commentary:

"The English are making frantic endeavours to enlist the sympathies of the young people of these islands on behalf of their overgrown Empire. But the trend of modern politics is, fortunately, in exactly the opposite direction to that in which the friends of 'expansion' would like us to oblige the minds and consciences of our children to proceed". *11

Erskine's strategy was adopted from Sinn Fein in Ireland.Hence though by 1914 he was advocating Federal Home Rule, by the end of World War 1 he had moved to a position of complete independence, which he maintained for the rest of his life. His overall importance was as an advocate-cum-propagandist for the national movement generally and Gaelic revivalism particularly. He saw Gaeldom's future as inextricably linked to the progress of Scottish self-rule initiatives, which were then at an early stage. Erskine shared the faith of such Irish counterparts as Eamonn De Valera, Douglas Hyde and Eoin MacNeill, none of whom saw any future for the native tongue under Crown rule. Also, all lamented the negative image of Gaelic, as symbolising a suppressed nation, and thus believed that any national resurgence should revive the Gaelic identity.

William Gillies proved to be a sound organiser, whose efforts gave the SNL a viable corporate existence. Like Erskine, Gillies had spent time in Ireland, and later served an apprenticeship as an organiser with the Highlands Land League. At the time of the Easter Rising (April 1916), he was among the few non-Irish to support the initiative. Following his return to a business career in London, Gillies worked assiduously to advance his message within Gaelic and ex-patriate Highland organisations, speaking at countless meetings and distributing literature. Eventually in february, he organised the first London branch of the Scots National League. Thereafter other branches emerged, and a limited amount of publicist activities resulted in the early 1920s.

It is beyond the scope of this book to trace the activities of nationalist organisations, except in so far as they relate to Gaelic language politics in either country. The Scots National League, as Brand recounts, was significant for its advocacy of Gaelic revivalism, and rather little else.*12 It wielded only a minor impact on the embryo Scottish nationalist movement that was then experiencing its birth pangs, as well as the wider debate on Scotland's future. The League eventually merged with other nationalist groups to form the National Party of Scotland in 1928, from which the modern Scottish National Party (SNP) emerged in 1934. In terms of legacy, the SNL's self-anointed role as "keeper of the Gaelic conscience" ensured a place for Gaelic in future nationalist programmes; a significant factor in later decades when Gaelic issues entered the public domain.

Although the period 1920-65 was generally a poor one for Scottish Gaeldom, nevertheless from the late 1950s onwards there were occasional stirrings in Scottish public life that provided grounds for hope. These were mainly concentrated in the media and education, and came about partly as a result of assiduous lobbying by groups like An Comunn Gaidhealach, partly a positive social climate in the mid-1960s, and partly a mini-nationalist revival occurring over the same period. The full effects were felt in Westminster elections by the early and mid-1970s.

From the late 1930s/early 1940s onwards, there had occurred a modest Gaelic renaissance in the literary world, with publication of the celebrated poetry of Sorley Maclean (Somhairle MacGill-Eain) and George Caimbeul Hay (Deorsa Mac Iain Dheorsa) in various themes, styles and forms. This resurgence further extended to Gaelic drama, leading to the formation in1952 of the Gaelic literary magazine, Gairm. In 1958, there began the introduction of Gaelic Medium instruction to select primary schools in bilingual areas. This scheme was of a pioneering kind with limited short-term effects, but enabled further developments in subsequent decades, especially in Hebridean schools.

Gaelic broadcasting experienced a slow birth, with the introduction in 1959 of a three hour weekly slot on BBC Home Service Radio (later Radio Four). The latter increased to four hours in 1970, and as shown in Chapter 3, broadcasting developments went from strength to strength over ensuing decades. Elsewhere, increased grant support from the Highlands and Islands local authorities enabled An Comunn Gaidhealach to appoint a full-time professional director and public relations officer in 1965. In 1966, Glasgow University, with public aid, published a Gaelic historical dictionary, with further developments in Gaelic literature following over the next four years.

Generally, by 1966, the year when Harold Wilson's Labour administration received a decisive working majority in the March election, the position of Scotch Gaeldom appeared uncertain. Native-speaking numbers were at their lowest ever, while the Gaidhealtachd had contracted principally to the Outer Hebrides, and even there was experiencing the encroachment of anglicising forces in education, commerce and the media. Although some developments had occurred in broadcasting and Gaelic publishing, both were in short supply, while Gaelic medium education had moved no further than the experimental stage.Political sponsors were scarce, given the paucity of votes available to any party from the Gaidhealtachd. Additionally, there was the problem of low esteem, which inhibited the efforts of the most redoubtable reformers in education, media and publishing.

The next fifteen years were to prove crucial to the survival bid of Scottish Gaels and their allies in the political, educational and cultural fields.

NORTHERN IRELAND; It has already been shown in Chapter 1 how the Unionist character of the Northern Irish state made Gaeldom's prospects look bleak from the outset in 1921.

Hostility towards the Gaelic language and culture by successive Unionist administrations was partly due to the Unionist sense of political Britishness, which Gaelicism's historic legacy contradicted.More particularly, the association of Gaeilgeoir lobbyists with Sinn Fein, as in the south, had made them synonymous in Unionist eyes. Hence for the fifty years of its existence, Stormont pitted its resources and authority against the culture of Gaeldom. No cognisance was taken of the historic roots of the language nor its Scottish dimension, with which many Protestants would have otherwise identified. Quite simply, Gaeldom was treated as a subversive culture, unwelcome in the state schools, effectively blacked out of state broadcasting, and denied both recognition and public funding for its arts and cultural projects. The 1949 Public Health and Local Government

Miscellaneous Provision Act (N.I) made illegal the use of Irish in street names. Hence Gaelic dependence on Nationalist political sponsorship proved to be a necessity, since only in that quarter were support and recruits to be found. Various academic observers like Brendan O'Leary and John Mc Garry, Paul Bew, Richard Rose and Henry Patterson have all noted the Nationalist exclusion from power in the Northern Irish state during the Stormont years.*13

However, Stormont's negative effects on the Irish language and culture have not been traced with the same precision; thus lending an extra dimension to this inquiry. The latter needs to be examined in the various areas of educational, cultural and broadcasting life, and compared with the experiences of the Scottish Gaelic lobby around the same era.

An example of the anti-Gaelic attitude prevailing among the Unionist hierarchy came in a Stormont speech from the then Prime Minister, Viscount Craigavon, on 24th March, 1936. On that occasion, he was defending the termination of a small grant for the teaching of the language in schools, but the wider prejudices of the Unionist establishment were made apparent:

"What use is it, in this busy part of the Empire, to teach our children The Irish language? What use would it be to them? Is it not leading them along a road which has no practical value? We have not stopped the teaching; we have stopped the grants, which I think have amounted to £1,500 a year. We have stopped the grants simply because we do not see that these boys being taught Irish would be any better citizens." *14

Unionist hospitality betrayed an ignorance of Gaeldom's place in the cultural heritage of the North of Ireland. As early as 1795, a Gaelic magazine, Bolg an tSolair, had functioned in Belfast, while the Belfast Harpers Society and Ulster Gaelic Society each provided events in the native medium. Significantly, reliable accounts from historians like O'Snodiagh and O'Fiaich suggest that late nineteenth century Northern Gaelic revivalism was prevalent among liberal Presbyterians, who constituted the largest educated group of those times, and were in any case more conscious of the Scottish dimension than later generations of Orange leaders would have wished.*14

Conradh na Gaeilige (Gaelic League) had a thriving Belfast branch from its earliest days, which composed an executive of mainly nationalistic Presbyterians and a largely Catholic ordinary membership.*15 So was the first Belfast Feis held in 1900. In the early 1900s, Catholics flocked into Belfast from the west Ulster counties in search of work, a factor that influenced the city's political demography in the short and long terms. However, it was Orangeism that impeded popular Gaelicism from growing among working class Protestants. The latter's dogged adherence to Unionism was underlined by a hostility to the Irish language; a trait imposed by the Stormont regime on Northern educational, cultural and political life throughout its hegemony years.

It was in the field of education that the greatest hostility was experienced by Northern Gaeilgeoiri from Stormont. Unlike the new Southern state in 1922, where the teaching of Irish was adopted as a government priority conversely the Unionist administration in Belfast had no policy on the place of Gaelic in schools. However, the Gaelic League's Ard Scoil Ultach (Ulster College), founded in 1906 as Belfast's Irish medium Teacher Training College was refused recognition by the new Northern Ireland Ministry of Education. So too were its teaching certificates denied Ministry recognition. Moreover, the Celtic Studies professorship at Queens University, Belfast, which had not been filled since the death of John O'Donovan in 1861, was allowed to remain vacant until 1945. An application from the Catholic Bishops to make Irish a compulsory entry subject for R.C student teachers was refused by the Ministry in 1929. Significantly, it was not until the mid-1960s that Celtic Studies departments were created in St Mary's and St Joseph's Catholic Teacher Training Colleges, Belfast, thereby limiting their scope in schools over the preceding period.*15

Schools, specifically Catholic schools (which were state assisted but managed by the Church), were directly affected by Stormont's anti-Gaelic policies. State (Protestant) schools did not offer Gaelic in their curriculum, nor was it taught in the various Protestant grammar schools in Belfast and throughout Northern Ireland at any time during the Stormont years (1921-72), nor indeed beyond then. In April 1923, the Education Minister, Lord Londonderry, issued a circular entitled "Instruction in Irish in Public Elementary Schools in Northern Ireland'.*16 This directive limited the time for teaching the Gaelic language to one and a half hours per week, allowing it as an alternative to history, and restricting its usage as an ordinary subject to pupils of third grade and above. Irish Gaelic could also be taught as an extra subject outside school hours to children of the third grade and higher, and fees would be paid to qualified teachers who gave at least forty hours of Irish classes as an extra subject per annum.*17 However, in 1926, the teaching of Irish as an extra subject was further restricted to grades V, V1 and V11 (Primary Schools), which effectively restricted learning to senior classes, thereby impeding the Gaelic League's efforts at encouraging Catholic schools to teach Gaelic from early years.

1926 also saw the withdrawal of the grants for the teaching of Irish as an extra subject at third and fourth grades. In that same year, Conradh na Gaeilige permitted the formation of an autonomous, albeit affiliated Northern division, Comhaltas Uladh, whose job it was to devise policies and negotiate for the interests of Ulster Gaeldom within the Six Counties. Seven years later, all special grants for Irish teaching were withdrawn by the N.I Ministry of Education. When in february 1927, the Education Minister refused a Comhaltas Uladh delegation's request to lower the introduction of Irish to classes below the third grade, he justified it on the grounds that Gaelic was a dying language in the Six Counties.*18 By 1933, according to the estimates of Maguire, some 10,500 Northern children were learning Gaelic at primary school, which amounted to 14% of Catholic pupils, and 5% of the total primary school population.*19 The ostensible reason given for the removal of the grant was the heavy financial commitments on the public purse.However, the Parliamentary Secretary, Mr Robb, also opined that the primary school was not an appropriate place for the teaching of Irish, and further suggested that many Catholic schools had not availed of the grant.*20 Robb's statement, alongside Prime Minister Craigavon's 1936 anti-Gaelic Stormont speech (earlier mentioned), underlined the political hostility of Ulster Unionism towards the Gaelic language and culture in Northern Ireland.

Unionist hostility was further pitted against Gaelic games, which were denied public sponsorship and effectively kept off the screens of BBC Northern Ireland and Ulster Television until the late 1960s.So also were Ceilidh dancing and Irish music similarly curtailed, while Gaelic arts and drama were kept to the periphery without official funding. This treatment of Irish culture by the Stormont establishment contributed to the Nationalist alienation, a phenomenon observed by various journalists and political scientists throughout the 1960s. One long term effect was to ensure Ulster Gaeldom's dependence on nationalist political sponsorship, while Gaelic cultural activities, including the Irish language, games and arts were fostered through the Catholic schools and voluntary organisations like Comhaltas Uladh and Cumann Luthchleas Gael (Gaelic Athletic Association). Indeed, as Jennifer Todd observed, Gaelicism formed part of the cultural life of the North's Nationalist community throughout the Stormont years and for long afterwards.*21 Specifically this meant that Gaelic sports clubs, Gaelic language groups, Ceilidh music and Gaelic arts associations predominated in Nationalist areas, as well as being actively promoted by the Catholic Church and in Catholic schools. The latter especially became cradles of Gaelic culture, and their contribution to maintaining a Gaelic identity, with only the minium of resources in a jurisdiction whose civil authority veered between indifference and hostility, has been accorded scant acknowledgement by political scientists. It is significant that the former Stormont Nationalist groups were the only political sponsors of Ulster Gaeilgeoiri, assisted by occasional interventions by the Southern government.

Nor had this situation fundamentally altered by the 1980s or 90s.The SDLP (Social Democratic and Labour Party), Sinn Fein and Catholic Church are principal sponsors for the language to a Northern Ireland Office that - as shown in ensuing chapters - is less hostile, but only marginally less indifferent than the preceding Stormont regime.

From the mid-1930s onwards, voluntary Gaelic organisations took a more active role in ensuring the survival of both language and culture. This was at the same time as the few remaining native Gaelic speakers in the Sperrins,Tyrone and Rathlin Island were gradually dying off, and with their demise (complete by the 1950s) went vital elements of indigenous Ulster Gaeldom.

Additionally, there was a small Gaeltacht in Omeath, North Louth, with a historic Ulster connection, where native speakers remained until the 1980s.*22 However, only the Donegal and Omeath Gaeltachtai remained for native Ulster speakers after 1955, along with Comhaltas Uladh and its sister Gaelic organisations.By 1983, the Omeath Gaeltacht had effectively gone with the death of the last native speakers.

Notwithstanding the hostile political climate, the Ulster Gaelic League (ie. Comhaltas Uladh) proved to be a remarkably obdurate body, and managed to meet various challenges facing the language.First among those was funding Irish teaching in primary schools..Comhaltas Uladh raised money by voluntary effort, as well as receiving occasional grants from the Dublin government, enough to partially meet the shortfall caused by the withdrawal of the Northern Ireland government grant. The Comhaltas also sought to popularise Irish learning by way of youth scholarships and Summer schools in the Donegal and Omeath Gaeltachtai, along with organising voluntary language classes, publishing learner materials and associated educational activities.Additionally, each year, Comhaltas organised a series of Feiseanna (competitions in Gaelic music, singing, dancing, conversation, history and games, similar to the Mods of Scottish Gaeldom) in every Ulster county. Over time, these events acquired substantial popularity, with the Feis an Duin (held at Newcastle, Co Down), Feis na Gleann (held at Waterfoot, Glens of Antrim), and Feis Bheal Feirste (Belfast) all becoming lead dates in the cultural calender of Northern Nationalists from the mid-1930s onwards. Significantly, these annual events retain their mass popularity into the 1990s.

Comhaltas Uladh continued to lobby the Stormont Ministry of Education for concessions, but to little avail. The 1920s grant for renumerating Gaelic teachers tutoring outside school hours was not restored in the 1940s or '50s, nor was there any relaxation of limits on the teaching of Gaelic within the school curriculum.Moreover, Comhaltas Uladh's bid to have its Irish colleges teaching certificates recognised by the Ministry failed.

In the late 1940s and '50s, Comhaltas Uladh enjoyed modest success at regenerating a measure of Gaeilgeoir cultural activity in West Belfast. A series of voluntary language classes took root in the community, attracting several thousand adult learners. Other ancillary groups emerged, such as a Gaelic cycling club, with its own magazine, Roth (Wheel). There was also a Gaelic swimming club, two Catholic prayer groups,"Cuallact Mhuire" and "Realt", both of whom held their meetings in Irish. A Gaelic writers club existed, Cleit, while a Gaelic drama group also emerged in the mid-1950s, and Belfast Gaelic choir performed regularly at the Welsh Eistedfodd over the same period. The long term affiliation of a new Gaeilgeoir community augmented the Comhaltas profile, thereby ensuring the language's survival and subsequent resurgence in an urban environment. This in turn sowed the seeds for the Shaws Road and Bunscoileanna initiatives in 1970/'80s Belfast, which are examined in ensuing chapters.

The role of An Ard Scoil Ultach (Ulster College), situated near to Belfast city centre, assumed special significance over this period. In effect, it became principal centre for the propagation of the Ulster Gaelic dialect, and as such complicated the special aims of Comhaltas Uladh in keeping alive that same variant. Previously, the presence of Southern teachers in many Belfast schools, whose tutoring was in the Connacht and Munster dialects, raised fears among some Belfast Gaeilgeoiri about the future recognition of Ulster's distinctive Gaelic traditions. The Ard Scoil and Comhaltas Uladh ensured that such concerns were addressed. Moreover, the special contribution of Cumann Chluain Ard (the largest Gaelic League branch in Belfast) augmented the process with its vibrant Gaelic learning and social programmes.

Maguire's account of Belfast Gaeilgeoiri cites the 1950s 'Fal' group, who were to the forefront of so many local Gaelic activities.*23 This was a loose collection of Gaeilgeoir individuals, whose zest for the language led them to form several of the contemporary Gaelic groups previously mentioned. Their monthly journal, Dearcadh, acted as a forum for the group, as well as an outlet for their frustrations. One such concern was the absence of a national Irish language press anywhere in the country, lamented in the Dearadh issue of August 1954. Interestingly the remedy for this gap came from a quarter of a century later in Belfast, as will be seen in later chapters. Maguire further noted a gathering belief among several participants towards the close of the decade over the need for developing a permanent Gaeltacht community, with its own social and economic infra-structure. Without social and economic self-reliance, Belfast's Gaelic survival looked unlikely. This view was fashioned by observations of the efforts of community leaders at attracting jobs and industry to the Donegal Gaeltacht. In later decades there was a special appreciation of the endeavours of Donegal priest, Fr Lames Mac Dwyer, whose labours at spearheading fishing and farming co-operatives aroused national press attention. Besides, the creation of a Southern Gaeltacht ministry in 1956, augmented the growing sense of awareness among Gaeilgeoiri everywhere that Gaeltacht life needed viable economic roots and distinctive social institutions in order to survive.

Accordingly, among the 'Fal' group, attempts were made at generating some kind of economic infra-structure, albeit with poor success. An Irish credit union functioned briefly, as did an Irish medium shop. One member sold his business in Belfast, and invested the profits in establishing a new craft business in the Donegal Gaeltacht, which failed. When no financial rescue was forthcoming, the project ended in disillusionment and bitterness. Yet Maguire argues that those setbacks served to strengthen the Gaelic cause in the long term by their sheer obduracy.

*"Each achievement, whether long-term or fleeting, each plan which remained on some committee table, each unsuccessful attempt, represented, at the least, a contribution to a community's self-assertion of its Irishness. They prevented the ideal of an Irish-speaking nation from slipping into oblivion. Sometimes it was propelled forward. Sometimes it was just kept ticking over. It never quite died. What Irish speakers were determined to prove to themselves and to others was that the Irish language was a viable and satisfying medium of communication in today's society."**24

In reality, by 1965, only in West Belfast was there any growth in Ulster Gaeilgeoiri activity. Elsewhere the picture was one of pessimism about the language's future, both for the surviving Gaeltacht and for Gaelic learners. The Ulster Gaeltachtai had been greatly diminished over the preceding forty five years since partition, and no longer functioned as a living entity within the Six Counties. The latter was due partly to political hostility from the Belfast Unionist regime, partly to education neglect, and partly the chronic local economy in Gaeltacht areas, which had caused population defections and boosted English as the language of the new economy. So too did Gaeldom suffer from the political divisions that restricted Irish culture to Northern Ireland's Nationalist community. Only in a very limited way did Ulster Gaeldom benefit from the mini-resurgence that was slowly effecting improvements for their Scottish brethren in radio broadcasting, education, publishing and public funding.

Yet even the unpromising Sixties contained green shoots that augured cautiously for a better future for Gael Uladh. There was growing Gaeilgeoiri momentum for developing a new urban Gaeltacht in West Belfast(as earlier described), which blossomed over the ensuing twenty years. On the educational front, the combined O ' level (GCSE after 1986) and A level GCE language entries for Northern Ireland schools showed Irish Gaelic entries at 1,163 in 1960 and 1,624 in 1965. In both instances Irish was the second most popular language behind French, and more popular than German and Spanish.*25 Significantly, this position sustained itself over the ensuing thirty years, thereby generating demand for Gaelic teaching, resources provision, and the training of Irish teachers. The mid-1960s also saw the opening of Celtic Studies departments at St Mary's and St Joseph's Training Colleges, Belfast, which offered better prospects for meeting Irish teaching demands in Northern Ireland's Catholic schools.

The mini-resurgence in Irish language activity had been strengthened by developments in other areas of Northern Gaelic culture.Not least among these was the success of Northern counties in the All-Ireland senior Gaelic football competitions, with Armagh and Derry reaching the 1953 and 1958 finals respectively, and Down's near-legendary "Sixties babes" winning the hallowed Sam Maguire Cup(the first Northern county to win the premier trophy) in 1960, 1961, and 1968.Other more modest successes followed throughout the same decade for the junior and minor football teams of Fermanagh, Derry and Tyrone, while the junior and intermediate hurlers of Antrim and Down also broke through at national level.Given the mass popularity of Gaelic games among Northern nationalists, these successes injected a new confidence and assertiveness that was felt in the divided Six Counties, and welcomed throughout the rest of Ireland.

Gaelic sporting successes percolated to other areas of Northern Gaelic life, where positive waves were building.The emergence of an educated nationalist class from Queens University, Belfast by the early 1960s, along with the growth of television and early civil rights agitation, all contributed to a new momentum. This climate was to transform the character of Northern nationalism over ensuing decades. Given the proximity of Northern Gaeilgeoiri to political nationalism, the ensuing phenomena of the Seventies and Eighties defined a juncture from which Gael Uladh could not fail to be affected.

FOOTNOTES & REFERENCES

1. *See U.K Census figures, 1931-61; also cited in V McKee, Contemporary Politics (1995), p.94*

2. *See (i)MaKinnon (1991); Chaps.4, 5 &6. (ii) Withers (1984); Chaps.7 &8.*

3. *Brand (1978) ;Chap.11, pp.182-190.*

4. *Ibid.*

5. *See*

Hugh MacDiarmid, 'The Caledonian Antisyzygy', The Modern Scot (vol.2 No.2, January 1932); and Jack Brand's appraisal of MacDiarmid, Brand (1978), Chap.6.

6. *James Hunter; The Making of the Crofting Community, Chaps 5,9 10, 12 (Glasgow,1976).*

7. *Brand (1978); Chap. 11, pp, 182-188.*

8. *Brand (1978); Chap. 11, pp,182-183.*

9. *Brand (1978); Chap.11, p. 183.*

10. *Guth na Bliadhna; all issues 1904-1920.*

11. *Guth na Bliadhna; Vol.2 No.1, p.28.*

12. *Brand (1978); Chap 11, pp.182-188.*

13. *See (i) Brendan O'Leary & John MCGarry; The Politics of Antagonism; Understanding Northern Ireland (1993, Oxford).*

(ii) Paul Bew and Henry Patterson; The British State and the Ulster Crisis: From Wilson to Thatcher (1985,London).

(iii) Richard Rose; Northern Ireland: A Time of Choice (1976 London)

14. *(i) Tomas O'Fiaich ; 'The language and political history'; in Brian O'Cuiv (Ed); A View of the Irish Language,(1969, Dublin Sationary Office). (ii) P.O'Snodaigh; Hidden Ulster (1973, Belfast).*

15. *Gabrielle Maguire; Our Own Language:An Irish Initiative Chap 2,(1990, Belfast /Clevedon). (An authoritative study of the Gaeilgeoir community in West Belfast, based on Dr Maguire's earlier Ph.D thesis on that subject, Queens University, Belfast.)*

16. *File Ed. 13/1/878; Public Records Office, Northern Ireland.*

17. *Ibid.*

18. *File Ed. 13/1/516; Public Records Office, Northern Ireland.*

19. *Figures cited in Maguire (1990); Chap.3, p.43.*

20. *Northern Ireland Parliamentary Debates; Commons,Vol.xv, Col. 1077, 25th April, 1933.*

21. *Jennifer Todd; 'Nationalist Political Culture in Northern Ireland'; Paper presented to the U.K Political Studies Association Conference, 12-14th April, 1988,Plymouth Polytechnic.*

22. *The Omeath Gaeltacht was historically linked to the Ulster Gaelic tradition, and thus its dialect was that of Ulster.Although modern day Louth is a county of Leinster, in earlier times North Louth formed part of the historic province of Ulster, thereby linking its former Gaeltacht to Gael Uladh.*

23. *Maguire (1990); Chap.2 ,p.31.*

24. *Maguire (1990) ; Chap.2.pp.31 &32.*

25. *Figures cited in Maguire (1990) ; Table 1, Chap.3, p.46.*

CHAPTER 3
GAELDOM'S MINI-RENAISSANCE 1965-85

Introduction: Evidence presented in Chapter 2 shows that after sinking to a low ebb in the inter-War years, the fortunes of Scottish and Irish Gaels slowly improved after 1950.Notwithstanding the diminution of the Scottish Gaidhealtachd and near-disappearance of the Ulster Gaeltacht outside Donegal, by 1965 green shoots had begun to appear. Though tenuous, especially in Northern Ireland, those developments were sufficient to augur positively for the survival, if not total recovery of the Gaelic language in both countries.

The key to survival was Gaeldom's incorporation within the educational systems and civic cultures of each country.In the process, Gaelic made headway as a language of broadcasting, cultural projection and specialist literature. The Gaelic survival and its application to education and wider culture made necessary initial government recognition and funding. In that respect, the different images of Gaelic in Scotland and Northern Ireland, along with their political sponsors, proved to be of prime importance in determining the attitudes of public policy makers, and ultimately the government. This helped shaped the fortunes of the language differently in the two countries. The relatively apolitical lobby of An Comunn Gaidhealach and its sister organisation in Scotland ensured a positive response from the Scottish Office, with appropriate benefits following over ensuing decades.Conversely, the anti-Gaelic prejudices of Northern Ireland's Unionist establishment forced Gael Uladh into continuing reliance on Nationalist sponsorship, which limited both its appeal and funding.

However, as the 1970s and '80s were times of Nationalist resurgence, given Gaeldom's prominence in popular Nationalist culture, it too was elevated in profile and government recognition.

Significantly, its place in Northern Ireland's civic society underwent gradual reappraisal in the direction of inclusion and rising esteem.

This chapter poses two questions, both of prime relevance to developments occurring over this period.Neither carry conclusive answers, but both merit consideration against the general background of developments for Scottish and Ulster Gaeldom.

First, how far was the Gaelic mini-renaissance a product of the natural evolution of events, stretching back to the 1930s Gaelic literary revival in Scotland? The same question pertains to the 1950s Gaeilgeoir resurgence in Belfast and cultural revival elsewhere in the Six Counties of Northern Ireland ? Second, to what degree was the mini-renaissance in both countries fashioned by the new liberal political climate of the late 1960s/70s?

Was Gaeldom a beneficiary of the same international tide that rendered civil rights for American blacks, scorned the U.S bombing of Hanoi, and encouraged a humanitarian perspective of Nigerian Ibos' forlorn quest for Biafra?

Attempts at casting light on those questions require an examination of the cultural influences underpinning Sixties social developments.In particular, connections between minority cultures and Schumacher's "..small is beautiful" theory merits assessment, as does the link between political and cultural rights within the British constitutional jurisdiction

With the benefit of hindsight, it may be said that the Sixties liberal climate encouraged a generous view of Gaeldom's claims to a greater share of educational, arts and cultural resources. Additionally, it may be noted that the same period generated a greater open-mindedness by sections of Northern Irelands administrative establishment towards the culture, if not language of Gaeldom. This shift of emphasis occurred during the liberal - albeit ill-fated - premiership of Terence O'Neill, with its policy of civic inclusion.It is noted for the modest success of Gaels in making modest inroads to broadcasting and higher education. The impact and consequences of O'Neills policies have been debated by contemporary historians, and indeed it is not universally accepted that he was speaking to accommodate Nationalism, as more kill it off by kindness.*1 Moreover, as was shown by Bernard Conlon's thesis on American influence over Northern Ireland's civil rights movement, assertions of political liberties translated into demands for parity of esteem for suppressed cultures.*2 This demand was initially heard during the late 1960s, but had to await the 1985 Anglo Irish Accord before acquiring quasi-legislative status.Meanwhile, the Ulster Gaelic lobby was left striving for whatever limited concessions could be extracted from a reluctant Stormont administration, under Unionist and - following Direct Rule's introduction in March 1972 - Westminster mastery.

An examination of the experiences of both Gaelic lobbies shows the apolitical Scottish Gaels to have gained most from a British state that did not feel confronted by the agenda of its political sponsors. Therein lay the greatest difference between the two wings of Gaeldom, something imposed by the events of history.

Scotland: The advances made by Scottish Gaeldom over the years 1965-85 occurred on several fronts. They represented a triumph for the patient lobbying of An Comunn Gaidhealach over the previous years, whose efforts had contributed to a growing climate of positive opinion towards Gaelic by various sections of the Scottish political and public sector establishment.

The new climate had been long in coming, but was evident by the late 1960s.Its manifestations emerged in the fields of education, broadcasting, publishing, the environment and local government.

Significantly, it was assisted by a sympathetic, if also cautious Scottish Office, whose pro-Gaelic policy was continued under successive Labour and Conservative governments. Doubtless the political neutrality of An Comunn Gaidhealach, and its insistence on maintaining a strict distance from party sponsorship boosted its credibility as a sectional lobby group. The A.C.G lobby encouraged various corporate institutions to re-appraise previous indifference to the language. As a result, by 1980 all four Scottish parties - Labour, Conservatives, Liberals and the Scottish Nationalists - had adopted positive policies on Gaelic and its place in Scottish society. This domestic 'consensus' was to prove an invaluable aid towards later A.C.G. campaigns for the Scottish Office funding of Gaelic medium education in the Highlands and Hebridean Gaidhealachd.So too did it strengthen A.C.G in its representations to local authorities, broadcasters, churches and schools for greater priority for Gaelic in their respective areas. Such lobbying might have proved more difficult had the language been closely associated with political nationalism, as in Northern Ireland. Yet the absence of a political dimension also leaves Scottish Gaeldom rather dependent on the good will of the Scottish Office and associated civic and corporate sectors.

As will be shown later in this chapter, by joining forces with the Scottish Office and local authorities, An Comunn Gaidhealach risked losing something of its erstwhile independence.This transition pertains to what Wyn Grant - writing on pressure groups - defines as the "insider" versus "outsider" group scenario.*3 Grant argues that while groups benefit from public sector favour through policy advantages, they also lose their detachment, and become tied to the very establishment on whose patronage their raison d'etre depends. This can lead to internal rifts, and the charge of "compromise", which in turn may generate secessions and the formation of revival groups. While A.C.G was spared the most extreme experiences, nevertheless its edge got blunted, thereby leading to occasional internal frictions and the founding of a short-lived rival campaigning group.

Notwithstanding the alternate strategies of radicalism versus co-operation, an examination of Gaeldom's advances over the period shows an impressive level of progress.

One area of major advancement occurred in broadcasting.Gaelic schools broadcasts commenced in 1970, and by 1975 BBC TV

Scotland was providing a modest quota of musical, current affairs, religious and drama programmes. In 1979, BBC Scotland commenced the long-running Gaelic learners series,'Can Seo', which was undertaken in co-operation with An Comunn Gaidhealach, and from which learner tapes were produced and marketed throughout Scotland and beyond. The two IBA companies in the Highlands and Islands, STV and Grampian Television, also raised their profiles by opening studios in Stornoway.That same year (1979) saw the formation of Radio Nan Gaidheal, with studios operating from Stornoway, Inverness,Skye and Glasgow. The radio initiative was aimed at servicing the needs of each Gaelic community. It also squared with a positive new climate among broadcasters, favouring provision for minority cultures.

Gaelic publishing was another beneficiary of the period.Following publication in1966 of Glasgow University's Gaelic historical dictionary, with public aid, other developments followed. In 1969, the Wilson government redeemed a pledge to provide annual subsidies for Gaelic books, with the creation of the Gaelic Books Council. One immediate effect of that particular initiative, as noted by Kenneth MacKinnon, was the publication of thirty seven new Gaelic titles in the Council's first year. This compared with a previous national average of three.*4 In 1970, the programme of state-aided Gaelic publishing took another stride forward, with the launching of the Highlands Book Club/Club Leabhar.Over the next ten years, the body produced seven Gaelic/English bilingual titles.Its successor is the Gaelic publisher, Acair, with a headquarters in Stornoway, Lewis.

Another related development area occurred in local government and environmental affairs.The Scottish Office lent crucial support to the 1969 Local Authorities (National Mod) Scotland Act, that began as a Private Member Bill from the liberal M.P for Inverness and Lochaber, Russell Johnstone, which empowered local Councils to offer discretionary grants towards aiding the National Mod. This reform was augmented by another, enabling Scottish local authorities in the Highlands and Islands to erect Gaelic road signs, with government assistance.However, the latter's value was undermined by the minimal take-up rate by Highlands local authorities over the ensuing period.

The creation of the Highlands and Islands Development Board (H&I.D.B) in 1975, with a briefing to stimulate the region's socio-economic regeneration through aiding economic and cultural projects, also proved beneficial to Gaeldom. For Gaelic organisations this meant grant provision for Gaelic publishing and other enterprises, thereby rendering the H&I.D.B and its successor organisation, Highlands and Islands Enterprises(H.I.E), invaluable patrons of Gaelic interests.*5 In 1984, the H.&I.D.B appointed a Gaelic Development Officer, and formulated a Gaelic Development policy.It provided financial assistance to Comhairle nan Sgoiltean Araich (Gaelic Playgroups Association) for the purpose of recruiting staff and acquiring a headquarters. The Board also funded the Gaelic Learners body, Comunn an Luchd-Ionnsachaidh, whose profile and capacity grew over ensuing years.

Several educational developments were initiated over the period. In 1972, a Gaelic vocational arts college opened on the Isle of Skye, Sabhal Mor Ostaig, which has since evolved into an advanced Scottish Further Education college. Additionally, over the past two decades the college has become a centre for conferences and Easter/Summer schools for Gaelic learners. Another significant development was the laying of foundations for the Gaelic Medium Education programme, which was funded by the Scottish Office, and developed in conjunction with An Comunn Gaidhealach. This entailed the creation of whole Gaelic teaching units in select schools in the Highlands and Hebridean Gaidhealtachd. It was aimed at ensuring continuity among mainly native speakers, whose children might otherwise have had an English medium education. Details of the programme appear in chapter 5, but it is worth noting that the plan was agreed in 1985, with the first Gaelic medium units opening the following year.*6

Perhaps the most significant development of the period occurred in 1975 in the Outer Hebrides, with the local government reforms originally initiated by the Heath government. In that year, from the previous division of the jurisdiction between Inverness and Ross-shire councils respectively, came a new single tier Gaelic purpose local authority, Comhairle nan Eilean (Western Isles Council) covering the entire Outer Hebrides.

Its administration centre was located at Stornoway, Isle of Lewis, and its boundaries squared entirely with those of the Western Isles Parliamentary Division.

Overseeing a population of 29,000 Comhairle nan Eilean emerged as the third smallest local authority in Scotland and the United Kingdom.

From that base, other significant developments followed in the promotion of Gaelic through education and a sympathetic community policy. The role of Comhairle nan Eilean - a uniquely Gaelic institution - is discussed more fully in Chapters 4 and 5. *7

Equally significant were political developments taking place over the period, which combined to boost the Gaelic resurgence and its acceptability to various wings of Scottish public officialdom.

The election of Donald Stewart (former Provost of Stornoway) as Scottish Nationalist MP for the Western Isles in June 1970 proved significant.

This was especially so, given Stewart's commitment to extending rights and facilities for Gaelic speakers. *8

In February 1981 Stewart produced the Gaelic (Miscellaneous Provisions) Private Member's Bill, which sought statutory recognition for Scottish Gaelic, as well as defining the right to Gaelic medium facilities, following the Welsh pattern. *9 Although falling to a Conservative filibuster - largely sponsored by Douglas Hogg - in fact many of its provisions have since been adopted. *10

The latter factor was noted by Stewart in his memoirs. *11

Also significant was the Scottish Conservative Party's positive embracement of the language. That this happened was due in no small way to the Tories' perception of the Gaelic lobby as politically innocuous, and thus deserving of modest aid. Indeed under Edward Heath's progressive leadership, a new mood of Tory multi-culturalism was on the ascendant among Party policy makers.

This enabled an accommodation to be made with An Comunn Gaidhealach and its sister bodies representing Gaelic interests in all walks of Scottish life. Thus the Wilson government's pro-Gaelic policy was continued by its Conservative successor, whose Scottish Secretary Gordon Campbell publicly affirmed his support on taking office in June 1970.

Doubtless Scottish Gaeldom's gradual incorporation into the educational and broadcasting system over the next twenty years had further encouraged Conservative acquiescence. Moreover, the position of Iain MacLeod - being of Lewis parentage - in Heath's Shadow Cabinet (MacLeod died suddenly within weeks of becoming Chancellor in 1970), served to augment the understanding.

One immediate benefit of Conservative goodwill was the new Scottish Office regime's agreement to fund a full-time Director for An Comunn Gaidhealach in the Outer Hebrides.

This appointment was agreed in 1971, and the Director operated from an office at Stornoway. Some fifteen years later, another publicly funded Gaelic organisation opened its doors in Inverness, Comunn na Gaidhlig.

This body was charged with co-ordinating the activities of various Gaelic sector groups in education, broadcasting, adult learners, Gaelic drama and arts. It has since emerged as something of an umbrella lobby group, acting as a combined voice for Scottish Gaeldom on various matters of education, the media and cultural status.

Bi-partisanship in Gaelic policy making proved beneficial because of continuity and a generous public purse. And the absence of Gaelic partisanship ensured that despite slow initiatives, reforms in education, broadcasting and the arts did not depend on the patronage of any single party in any single office. Indeed the situation prevailing in 1980, by which all major Scottish parties had adopted positive Gaelic policies, ensured that Gaelic was placed above the gladiatorial frictions of party rivalry.

This had the effect of elevating An Comunn Gaidhealach and later Comunn na Gaidhlig to the role of semi-institutional organisations in the Highlands, Outer Hebrides and Skye.

As public sector Gaelic investment increased ACG and CNG found themselves benefiting from the public purse and playing a major role in defining the character of Gaelic education, broadcasting and funding. While this development was inevitable, nevertheless the 'establishment' transition of ACG and sister organisations produced some tensions within the Scottish Gaelic movement by the mid-1980s. One consequence of the latter was the emergence of independent political lobby groups like Comunn na Canain Albanaich; a 1970s and 80s militant campaigning organisation modelled on the Welsh Language Society.

Other sectional groups like the Gaelic Playgroups Association and Gaelic Learners organisation are autonomous, self-managed and independent of the Gaelic 'establishment.'

Generally, whatever the price paid in lost independence, by 1985 the previous anglicisation of the Highlands and Hebrides had been halted. The Census figures for 1961-81, while showing a drop in the numbers of native speakers, nevertheless also indicated the decline to have slowed ie, 1961 - 80,620; 1971 - 88,892; 1981 - 79,307. *12

Significantly, Census figures overlook the increasing numbers of Gaelic second language speakers and learners whose purpose had been revived by various developments occurring over the period in focus.

While numbers of second language Gaels are hard to quantify, there is reliable data on the current number of Gaelic learners. According to a 1995 report by John M.K. Galloway, commissioned by Comunn na Gaidhig and supported by the Scottish Gaelic Learners Association/Comann an Luchd-Ionnsachaidh, there; are

8,000 Gaelic learners throughout Scotland. *13

A majority are located in the greater Glasgow area, among the second and third generations of migrant Hebrideans and Highlanders, with proportionate numbers found elsewhere in Scotland and among Scottish communities abroad. Quite how this figure stood over the period 1965-85 is impossible to ascertain, due to the absence of figures for that time.However, it is safe to suggest that the foundations for current patterns were rooted in those years of development. - See Appendix 2 for full details.

This expansion boosted the Gaelic profile, laying structural foundations for the development of Gaelic education, the arts, broadcasting and publishing. Those foundations enabled future developments, and in the process encouraged a new self confidence that came with the rising esteem characterising Scottish Gaeldom from the late 1960s onwards. If that progress had been achieved at the price of political independence, then given the increasing benevolence of the Scottish political and administrative establishment, it seemed like a price worth paying.

Northern Ireland: The progress of Gael Uladh was less promising than that of Gaidheal Albannaich over the period 1965-85. This situation was due to three reasons, all related to the political character of Northern Ireland in those years.

First was political polarisation and the resultant Unionist monopoly of power. Various studies by O'Leary and McGarry, Bew and Patterson and Rose (cited in Chapters 1 and 2) all examine the exclusion policies operated by successive Stormont governments against Nationalists. The latter extended to Nationalist culture, which included Gaelic sports, arts and the Irish language.

This had the effect of forcing Nationalists into campaigns of political - rather than cultural - assertion, of which the civil rights campaign, 1968-72, represented the most poignant example.

Second, Unionists at all levels of government were explicitly hostile to Nationalist aspirations and Irish culture, resenting the Irish identity as a threat to the Union and "....Ulster way of life."

Hence aside from the anti-Catholicism, so redolent of many Unionist sections, the scarcest regard was shown for Irish cultural pursuits, and none for the Gaelic language. After the imposition of Direct Rule in March 1972, the Northern Ireland Office proved an indifferent overseer of Gaelic interests, and almost as ungenerous as its predecessor with funding.

Only with the signing of the 1985 Anglo Irish Accord did a more positive attitude towards Gaelic emerge from the Northern Ireland administration, inclusive of new funding prospects.

Third, the Ulster Gaelic lobby was hampered by the absence of a traditional Gaeltacht within the Six Counties.

This situation marked a contrast to Scottish Gaeldom, where an established Gaidhealtachd existed in the Hebrides and Western Highlands. By contrast, Ulster Gaeilgeoiri pleas for funds and legal provision, emphasised heritage and cultural identity factors to a government body that was innately unsympathetic.

Over that same period there emerged green shoots augering cautious hopes among Ulster Gaeilgeoiri for the future.

In the main, these were more due to voluntary initiatives by Gaelic language and cultural activists than the active hand of government.

The period also witnessed a slow and often grudging, but unmistakable shift in official attitudes, such as enhanced the efforts of various Gaeilgeoiri operating under the umbrella of Comhaltas Uladh.

Given the language's place within a broad Irish cultural movement, that also encompassed Gaelic sports, music, drama and literature, it is noteworthy that language developments were accompanied by progress in all areas.

The effect was to boost both the confidence and self-reliance of Gael Uladh, sustaining it through the greatest ever political crisis afflicting Northern Ireland's divided and strained society since Ireland's partition in 1921.

The signs of that mini-resurgence were to be found on several fronts. As shown in Chapter 2, the opening of a Celtic Studies department in St Mary's and St Joseph's Catholic Colleges, Belfast, in the mid-1960's enabled the training of Irish language teachers to meet the growing demand from schools.

The Irish Studies Department at the New University of Ulster, Coleraine, opened in the late 1960's, offering degrees in Irish and other Celtic codes, thereby further augmenting Gaelic's progress within the Northern educational system.

Significantly over the ensuing two decades, Coleraine's campus required a positive reputation for hosting leading research, writing and advanced teaching in Irish and Celtic Studies.

The latter enhanced its standing to a level comparable with Celtic Studies departments in other universities in Ireland and Britain. Advances in higher education, while modest, served to boost the morale of Ulster Gaelic speakers.

Amongst other things, the latter indicated progress in the pursuit of parity of esteem for the Gaelic language and culture against the entrenched anglophile culture, so beloved of Unionist and British politicians.

Another significant development came in 1970 with a record 2,348 entrants for GCE 'Ordinary' and 'Advanced' level Irish Studies in Northern Ireland. Throughout the 1970's and 80's those figures remained consistently high, being second only to French, and commanding higher uptakes than German, Spanish or Italian (see Appendix 3 for details).

In 1969 initial corporate foundations were laid for what became Belfast's urban Gaeltacht. In that year the first Gaelic speaking family moved into a small housing site purpose-built by a local Gaeilgeoir development company, De Brun and Mac Seain Ltd in Shaw's Road, Andersonstown. Some assistance had been forthcoming from Comhaltas Uladh, but most funds were self-generated through voluntary channels. *14

The aim was to lay housing, educational and social infrastructures for the support of a native speaking community, most of whose families were drawn from among second language Gaels.

In Chapter 2 the background Beal Fheirste was examined, along with their organisation Teaghlaigh. Gabrielle Maguire's authoritative account of the Belfast Gaeltacht highlights its educational role, along with its steady growth over the ensuing 25 years. *15 Developments took two forms. First, in 1985 there a dozen families on the development (a figure that kept rising over the following decade) and this was accompanied by a general emergence of a viable community around Shaw's Road.

Second was the opening of the first Bunscoil - Gaelic medium primary school - in 1971. This operated independently for 13 years, before qualifying for Maintained status and funding from the North's Department of Education in 1984. The following year the original scoil had mushroomed into several similar institutions around Belfast, Derry and other Nationalist areas of Northern Ireland.

Chapter 5 carries a more detailed examination of Gaelic medium education and the Bunscoileanna movement, but its initial significance lies in the foundations laid during this period. *16

Another related development in Belfast was the launching in 1981 of La, the Irish language newspaper with a nationwide circulation. It began initially as a weekly but in 1984 became a daily, before distribution problems forced management in 1993 to revert to an enlarged weekly. *17 Maguire rightly notes that by 1985 it became a matter of pride to Ulster Gaeilgeoiri that notwithstanding all its disadvantages, in fact Belfast was publishing the only national newspaper in the native language. *18

As is shown an Chapters 4 and 5 La proved to be an important influence in the West Belfast Gaeltacht throughout the 1980's and 1990's. The paper actively sponsored Belfast's various educational and cultural initiatives while also serving as a publicist for the Gaeilgeoir community, whose esteem was boosted by positive profiles and sympathetic news coverage.

The period 1965-85 was also noteworthy for the slow opening up of Northern Ireland's broadcast media to Gaelic sports and culture.

The successes of Northern counties in national Gaelic Football and Hurling competitions - especially the Down football team who won three senior all-Ireland titles in the 1960's - boosted confidence among local Gaels, while strengthening demands for access to the airwaves.

By the late 1960's BBC TV Northern Ireland started showing limited highlights of top Gaelic Games, albeit only in peak summer season. Under pressure from a combined Gaelic sports lobby BBC NI provided second-half coverage of the 1968 Down v Kerry final. This created a precedent for the future when Gaelic sports coverage became more widespread both with BBC television and Radio Ulster (founded in 1975) and the independent stations, Ulster Television and Downtown Radio. All stations were providing a creditable results and match report service each week by 1977, with coverage of the top games. Yet it took another ten years before live television coverage of principal games were shown by which time Gaelic sport had become evermore integrated in Northern Ireland's cultural calendar.

While those developments represented a major advance on the pre-1965 position of little or no Gaelic sports on air, substantial gaps still existed. First, despite the popularity of Gaelic games among Northern Nationalists, and the presence of some 350 GAA hurling, football and camogie clubs in the Six Counties, media coverage never truly reflected the intensity of that activity. *19

While BBC, Ulster Television, and independent radio increased coverage in the early 1990's, with specialists recruited the inclusion of Gaelic Games and culture among "acceptable" broadcasting subjects was slow, grudging and countered by Unionist prejudices in its passage.

Second, Irish language coverage was exempted from the thawing process. By 1985 there were no regular Gaelic medium programmes of either a utilitarian or educational kind. Nor did the cultural activities - including musical fleadhs, ceili dancing festivals, Gaelic drama etc - of groups like Comhaltas Ceoilteoiri na hEireann (traditional musicians) receive broadcasting coverage.

This is was in marked contrast to the regular television coverage afforded to An Comunn Gaidhealach's National Mod by BBC Scotland and the independent broadcasters.

Third, Northern Ireland's broadcasters lacked any policy for providing a quota of programmes in the native language. This resistance prevailed despite the popularity of Irish in schools and both Northern universities, as well as the growing profile of Comhaltas Uladh and its sister groupings, who provided voluntary language classes at venues across Belfast and in rural towns. In that respect, the experiences of Ulster Gaeilgeoiri were less favourable than their counterparts in Scotland, who over the same period experienced real advances in broadcasting coverage.

Scottish broadcasters had shown a less grudging attitude towards An Comunn Gaidhealach's pleas for a Gaelic programmes quota and learners service.

Hence lines of distinction were clearly drawn between the two branches of Gaeldom.

It is significant that Gaelgeoir developments in Northern Ireland over the period 1965-85 were affected by the political and social upheavals then occurring. Civil rights marchers of the late 1960's and Nationalist parties like the SDLP and later Sinn Fein sought - amongst other things - parity of esteem for Irish culture within the civic environment of the North. *20

This included proportionate funding and legal entitlement for the Irish language in education, the media, cultural and community affairs, public administration and recognition by government.

Nationalists sought similar rights for Irish Gaelic from Stormont, and its Northern Ireland Office successors, as were deemed simultaneously accorded to Scottish Gaels by the Scottish Office. *21

The cultural parity question provided an issue for relentless agitation by Nationalists, with public funding and recognition of Gaelic culture challenging Northern Ireland Office claims to be operating a culturally even-handed policy.

Aside from central government the hostility of the Unionists towards the Gaelic language and culture, was clearly manifested through spiteful gestures by some local councils against Comhaltas Uladh, Cumann Luthchleas Gael and other Irish bodies.

Throughout the 1970's and 80's Councils in Belfast, Larne, Craigavon and Ballymena all refused grants and facilities for Gaelic Games, Irish language classes and cultural provision. The effect was to accentuate the resentment felt among Nationalists while ensuring a long-term priority for Gaelic causes on their political agenda.

The 1985 Anglo Irish Accord produced an historic admission from the British government to the legitimacy of Nationalist political aspirations. An extension of the latter was an acceptance of the need to remove past impediments to recognition and funding of the Irish language. To that extent, the Accord represented an advance on previous developments.

However, only the ensuing 12 years would show the Accord's real value to Gaeilgeoirism.

SUMMARY

In overall terms, the period 1965-95 witnessed many positive developments in the life of Gaels in Scotland and Northern Ireland.

Scottish Gaeldom had been principal beneficiary from a series of measures that boosted funding, outlets and entitlements to the language.In that respect, it had been aided by a liberal political climate, which looked benignly on the claims of historically disadvantaged groups. Moreover, the Wilson government (1964 -70) had a penchant for intervention and generosity with public funds, which provided a further advantage to Scottish Gaels.Conversely, Ulster Gaels made only limited headway. The Gaeilgeoir case being affronted by hostile Unionists in central and local government, it was thus linked by necessity to political nationalism.This meant its gains were limited to political progress achieved by Northern Nationalists.

Tactics also differed between the two Gaelic worlds.Scottish Gaels progressed by lobbyist techniques, primarily, though not exclusively through its chief representative group, An Comunn Gaidhealach. Priority was placed on forging positive attitudes; and these extended to politicians of all parties, newspapers, senior Scottish Office civil servants, broadcasters, publishers, educationalists, local government councillors and officers. Together, the sympathy of public administrators and opinion formers emerged throughout the 1960s and '70s to constitute a growing consensus, such as boosted the Gaelic profile in various areas of interest. This consensus provided a stable bedrock on which subsequent educational, cultural and environmental initiatives were founded.

By contrast, Ulster Gaels advanced their claims by a mixture of voluntary Gaeilgeoir initiatives and straightforward political assertiveness. They enjoyed no such consensus in Northern Irish society, many of whose chief public administrators and opinion formers were in any case Unionists, and thus hostile to Gaelic interests. Nor did they enjoy sympathy in the Northern Ireland Office, far less its Stormont Unionist predecessor. Accordingly, it was left to the growing confidence and organisational initiatives of Gaeilgeoiri in West Belfast and Gaelic sports/cultural activists elsewhere to ensure that Gael Uladh survived the hostility of an anglophile Northern establishment.Moreover, the emergence of an embryo Gaelic educational sector and urban Gaeltacht in Belfast was entirely due to independent Gaeilgeoir initiatives.The various offices of government proved unhelpful, and only tempered their hostility under pressures from an assertive Nationalist political campaign.

Scottish Gaeldom's progress, compared to the limited advances of its Ulster counterparts, was largely due to the former posing no challenge to the Scottish political establishment.Conversely, Gael Uladh was viewed by Unionists as the cultural wing of Irish republicanism, whose language and pursuits affronted their own anglophile outlook. Thus its only salvation lay with proving an appeal, and building viable political alliances, such as lent authority to the Gaeilgeoir agenda. The period 1965-95 saw some valuable openings occur in that direction.

FOOTNOTES AND REFERENCES

1. For an insight to the different perspectives held of the O'Neill premiership, see: (i) Johnathan Bardon - A History of Ulster (Belfast, 1992) (ii)Michael Farrell - Northern Ireland: The Orange State, (London 1976) plus O'Neill's own account of his premiership.

(iii)Terence O'Neill The Autobiography of Terence O'Neill: Prime Minister of Northern Ireland 1963-69 (London, 1972)

2. Bernard Conlon - The Northern Ireland Civil Rights Association: Comparative Perspectives Unpublished MA Dissertation, University of Ulster, 1984.

3. Wyn Grant - Pressure Groups, Politics and Democracy in Britain (London 1995.

4. MacKinnon (1991); p.104

5. MacKinnon (1991); Part 2, pp. 117-120.

6. Discussions and related documents - V. McKee/Donald John Maciver, Bilingual Educational Adviser, Comhairle nan Eilean; August 20, 1992, August 18, 1993, April 8, 1994, June 30, 1997.

7. V. McKee; Contemporary Politics (1995), Vol. 1, No 1, pp. 97-101.

8. Donald Stewart - A Scot at Westminster, Chapter 7, pp. 33-37. (Nova Scotia 1994).

9. MacKinnon; Part 2, p. 111.

10. Stewart (1994), Chapter 7, p. 35

11. Stewart,. Chapter 7.

12. See UK Population Census results, 1961, 1971 and 1981; HMSO.

13. John M.K. Galloway - Estimation of the Number and Distribution of Adult Learners of Gaelic; Final Report - commissioned by Comunn na Gaidhlig. (October 1995).

14. Maguire (1991); Chapter 5, pp. 67-75.

15. Maguire (1191); Chapters 4-7. The author is indebted to Dr Maguire for the value of her well researched book.

16. This author is indebted to An Chomhairle don Oideachas Lan-Ghaeilge (Council for Irish Medium Education), Gaeloiliuint, based in Belfast for its meticulous records. In particular Development Officer Cathail O' Donnaighle, and Education Officer Peadar MacMuirish, both provided much key information at short notice.

17. Interview - V. McKee/Gearoid O'Caireallain, Editor La, January 7, 1994.

18. Maguire (1991); Chapter 4, p. 102.

19. McKee; Contemporary Politics (1995), p.102.

20. See respective Westminster election manifestoes, 1983, 1987, 1992 and 1997, for the Social and Democratic Labour Party and Sinn Fein. Both explicitly supported the proper funding and access entitlements of Irish language bodies to education, the arts and community affairs.

21. Patsy McGlone - Gaelic Language and Culture: A Question of Identity, Irish News (Belfast) November 24, 1994.

CHAPTER FOUR
GAELIC IN THE COMMUNITIES
1985-97

By 1985 Scottish Gaels were enjoying comparatively generous funding for the promotional activities of voluntary groups and had made advances in the fields of Gaelic education with Scottish Office funding, but by contrast Irish Gaels, though allied to political Nationalism had achieved growth only through their own efforts.

The laying of the foundations for a Belfast Gaeltacht, along with the promoting of the language in schools and colleges, was augmented by the voluntary learners programme of Comhaltas Uladh and sister groups like Gael Linn and Glor na nGael. Even the sound media was opening up, while the slow rising fortunes of Cumann Luthcleas Gael and Comhaltas Ceoltoiri Eireann in Gaelic sports and music, enhanced the fortunes of Gael Uladh generally.

However though the 1970s and 1980s witnessed an easing of erstwhile government hostility, the more positive climate did not result in the release of abundant funds from the public purse.

This only happened with the advent of the Anglo Irish Agreement in 1985. The historic treaty ushered in a new era of recognition for Irish culture in the Six Counties by the British Government, with appropriate funding following later. Again the situation varied between the two Gaelic nations.

SCOTLAND: The years 1985-97 represented a consolidation of policy attainments achieved over the preceding twenty years. Significantly in most areas there occurred further developments.

The introduction of Scottish Office Specific Grants for Gaelic Medium Units, along with Government funding of Gaelic pre-school education formed the core policy of the 1990s. Both programmes were assisted by the contemporary climate favouring Gaelic interests, which generated the necessary political will for funding the policy.

Comhairle Nan Eilean's creation in 1975, as a Gaelic local authority along with other part-bilingual Highlands councils, augmented the process. It enabled professional co-ordination of legitimate community demand, thereby laying a basis for further development in the future.

Gaelic broadcasting continued its development from strides made in the 1970's and 80's. By 1991, there was a joint commitment between the BBC and the IBA to providing three hundred hours of Gaelic programmes per year. By 1995, Gaelic broadcasting had reached 375 hours per year, which included various cultural, religious, current affairs and Gaelic learners' programmes.

The long-running Can Seo series for Gaelic learners was repeated by BBC Scotland in Autumn 1993, and was followed by other learner programmes on IBA channels. Also, schools broadcasts provided a learners option, with follow-up tapes made available.

Gaelic broadcasting took a further step in the Autumn of 1992, when Scottish Television began the first Gaelic soap opera, Machair.

The use of established local artistes like the Gaelic singer and actor Simon MacKenzie from Harris, and Lewis actor Domhnull Ruadh, ensured the series' popularity throughout the Highlands and Hebrides.

More generally, greater television and radio coverage of culture succeeded in bringing leading Gaelic talents to national attention. Singers like Calum Kennedy (Lewis), Catherine Ann MacPhee (Barra) and Arthur Cormack (Skye), along with genial instrumentalist Blair Douglas, also from Skye, and the Gaelic rock group Runrig, were all marketed to appreciative audiences throughout Scotland and beyond.

So too did coverage of the National Mod and associated events offer younger Gaelic artistes the opportunity of recognition; with talented Lewis traditional singer Joanne Murray (a gold medallist in the 1996 Mod) and fellow islander Eilidh MacKenzie typifying those benefiting from the facility.

Even district choirs and local drama groups - both central to Hebridean community life - enjoy a profile from the extended media. One such beneficiary was Tong Gaelic Choir, Isle of Lewis. Its successes at the National Mods of 1988 and 1989 resulted in substantial media coverage, leading in turn to an invitation trip to Vancouver the following year, to compete in the local Mod. From the latter, a commemorative musical tape was produced. *1

At the ensuing 1991 National Mod, held in Dingwall, Tong Choir won five traditional ballad competitions, and were heavily profiled by the regional press and broadcast media. *2

Overall, the advent of Gaelic broadcast media - including Radio Na Gaidhlig and Gaelic programmes on mainstream channels - meant a desirable utility for sustaining the language. That utility included everyday language usage, as well as outlets for cultural talent, educational medium, public affairs debates and other Gaelic interests.

This had the further effects of raising the Gaelic profile, and projecting Gaelic culture to urban and Lowland Scotland. Additionally it enhanced the self esteem of Highlanders and Hebrideans in their indigenous language and cultural heritage. Doubtless the gathering climate of civic pride in Scotland's cultural heritage, that had become evident since the 1970s, aided the process. However, such advantages were sustained by the comprehensive programme of Gaelic expansion in the various areas of Scottish cultural life.

Gaelic arts also benefited from the new era. The National Gaelic Arts Project has been administered - with Scottish Office grant aid - from an office in Stornoway. Its main briefing was to act as a co-ordinator for various Gaelic drama and arts bodies, of whom Drama Naiseanta na h-Alba (DNA) is the principal youth group. There is also the professional Gaelic theatre company, Tosg, based at Sabhal Mor Ostaig, on the Isle of Skye, and funded by the Scottish Arts

Council. Its ever-growing media profile ensures yet another media outlet for Gaelic artistic talent and development. Additionally the Feisean (festivals of children's' Gaelic music and drama) are held across the Highlands, Hebrides and Glasgow. The rise in the Feisean ideal is underlined by the fact that in 1985 only two Feisean were held. These events popularise Gaelic music and arts among youth, providing an outlet for schools programmes and the talent pool of Gaelic choirs and drama companies. A special promotional organisation exists, Feisean nan Gaidheal, itself affiliated to the umbrella body, Comunn na Gaidhlig, and is publicly funded with an office and director.

Another dimension to Gaelic's rising public esteem is evidenced by the first ever scheduled appearance of Gaelic arts on the official itinerary of the 1997 Edinburgh International Arts Festival. Although Gaelic arts have long figured on the Edinburgh Fringe, elevation to official status for some six concerts augers well for the language's future cultural status and recognition.

Moreover, having a role at Edinburgh, however belated, implies recognition from the Scottish cultural establishment. The latter should guarantee Gaeldom's future status for educational, literary and artistic purposes, with all necessary funding and political acceptance underlining Gaeldom's broader incorporation within Scottish national culture.

Another development concerns the role of Gaelic in Highlands and Islands newspapers. Although no Gaelic newspaper exists on a scale comparable to La in Belfast, several papers have established Gaelic columns and support Gaelic activities in their respective communities.

Those publications include The Aberdeen Press and Journal, The Scotsman, The Oban Times, The Stornoway Gazette, West Highlands Free Press and Inverness Courier. Additionally the West Highlands Free Press, publishing in Skye, includes a monthly arts supplement, An Canan, while another monthly supplement, Guth na Gaidhlig, appears with the weekly Highland News.

Perhaps the greatest stimulus to Gaelic community development occurred in the Outer Hebrides through local government reform. The creation in 1975 of Comhairle Nan Eilean/Western Isles Council, provided a Gaelic authority for an area whose scattered population's historic dependence on crofting and fishing and the Gaelic language itself, boasted a homogeneous character.

Although by the 1970s crofting and fishing had diminished, their importance to the Hebridean economy and social infra-structure was and still, remains vital. Such factors have been accorded due recognition in James Hunter's authoritative history of the Hebridean crofters. *3

Additional factors have included the islands' unique geographical expanse; strong religious traditions among the Presbyterian majority and Catholic minority, along with the combined Hebridean population of 29,000, that makes Comhairle Nan Eilean among the smallest local authorities in Britain.

The population is mainly concentrated on Lewis. That dominance has provoked periodic tensions with the Southern Hebrides over issues such as health and educational resources distribution, but not to any profound degree. There is also the long-standing religious cleavage between Presbyterians and Catholics that flavoured Compton Makenzie's novel Whisky Galore. The sturdy Calvinist character of Lewis, Harris and North Uist is counterpoised by an equally staunch Catholicism in the less-populated southern Hebridean islands of Barra, Eriskay, South Uist and Southern Benbecula, thereby raising the potential for periodic confrontation. In fact, notwithstanding occasional strains, the experience has been one of compatibility. Given the active and assorted Presbyterian forces - including the Church of Scotland, Free Church and Free Presbyterians - that prevail in the Northern Hebrides alongside a durable Catholic fraternity, the avoidance of religious conflict ranks among Comhairle Nan Eilean's positive achievements over the years. It also reflects a healthy desire among most hebrideans to accept and work within their mixed community's parameters.

The approximate proportions of Gaelic speakers among the populated islands are as follows : Lewis has 70 per cent, Harris 85, Benbecula 75-80 (excluding military personnel), North Uist 80, South Uist 80, and Barra, Eriskay, Vatersay and Berneray 95. Other former Gaelic communities, such as Mingulay and the famous St. Kilda, have all been totally eroded by evacuations earlier this century. It should be added that the Lewis Gaidhealtachd is undermined by Stornoway's position as a largely English-speaking town. This factor renders Stornoway comparable to the Dublin of the past and its anglicised Pale. Furthermore, Stornoway's prominence in commerce, administration and education forces the rural Gaidhealtachd to conduct business in English, as well as offering little incentive to outsiders to respect Gaelic as the primary medium of communication. The English ethos has also had an assimilative effect on upcoming Gaels from the rural districts. Those factors might have damaged Gaelic interests more had not the new Comhairle Nan Eilean adopted a comprehensive bilingual policy, with preference accorded to Gaelic.

Comhairle Nan Eilean's front-line bilingual campaign was adopted from the beginning, and targeted three priorities. First was the Council's own Gaelic projection. A bilingual policy was formally adopted in April 1975, with a code of practice published in November 1977 and up-dated in October 1986.*4 This committed the Comhairle to providing Gaelic medium for all educational, social, environmental and cultural services. The overall goal was made clear in both languages from the outset:

"Is e run a phoilseasaidh "...gum bithdeadh Na h-Eilean siar na coimhearsnachd da-chananan co-labairt gus am bitheadh an rogha canain aif muinnyir an aite anns gach suidheachaidh".

"The general aim of the Council's policy is "...that the Western Isles should be a fundamentally bilingual community in which English and Gaelic are used concurrently as the languages of communication, that the

*people of the area can have the choice of language in as many situations as possible." *5*

In the Comhairle administration most staff are fluent Gaelic speakers. Notices and communications are provided in both languages, as are the full Comhairle, statutory committee meetings and interviews and correspondence. Actual deliberations of the Comhairle and committee meetings are undertaken in optional mediums, but with a preference for Gaelic. Additionally there is the special post of Bilingual Development Officer, who is at present Dolina MacLeod, a former Gaelic teacher and committed Gaeilgeoir. Mrs. MacLeod has responsibility for developing Gaelic primacy in Council affairs, plus the tedious task of ensuring translations of Council documents and notices. *6

Secondly Council environmental and tourist facilities are organised with the aim of projecting the Hebridean Gaelic character. Streets and roads have Gaelic names, as have Council buildings and institutions. The Council also encourages and assists local employers and voluntary groups, including the churches, to use Gaelic for their services and literature. Churches' attitudes vary considerably. The Free Church uses Gaelic for services, psalms and literature in Stornoway and the rural Gaidhealtachd. Others such as the Church of Scotland and the Free Presbyterians, hold optional gaelic services. The Catholic authorities in the Southern Isles have been positive, holding Gaelic masses in both churches in Barra, as well as Eriskay and South Uist. However only in Autumn 1992 did the Jesuit-run chapel at Stornoway begin holding a monthly Gaelic mass *7. Thirdly, priority has long been given to the promotion of Gaelic in Hebridean schools. Indeed, Gaelic education has proved to be a major plank in the Council's bilingual programme, especially with the recent drive towards the provision of Gaelic Medium units. More details about the application, funding and effects of this programme are offered in Chapter 5. Meanwhile it is appropriate to acknowledge that Gaelic education - of varying kinds - in the

Western Isles benefits from being located in Scotland's largest Gaidhealtachd, and promoted by the country's only Gaelic local education authority. Additionally in 1990 Comhairle established in its educational support service a Gaelic Resources database. This innovation was developed in liaison with other local authorities and Sabhal Mor Ostaig, and it was aimed at providing information on Gaelic resources and their availability to schools and colleges. By July 1997, the database held over 8,000 records on Gaelic books, videos, posters and music and had become a prime utility to public and voluntary bodies throughout Scotland's entire Gaelic sector.*8

Generally, Comhairle Nan Eilean has proved to be an effective generator of Gaelic educational and cultural interests. Although research inquiries revealed mixed feelings about the Comhairle among the Gaelic sectional groups, its record has in fact been positive in promoting the Gaelic language and championing Gaelic cultural interests in other ways. These have included hosting various international events for minority communities, including the 1990 conference at Stornoway for representatives from European minor language groups. Additionally, Comhairle Nan Eilean has been twinned with two bilingual Gaelic authorities in both parts of Ireland - Newry and Mourne Council in County Down, and Clare County Council in the South.*9 Moreover the Council has kept faith with its Gaelic policy, even in the embarrassing aftermath of the 1991 BCCI crash. Its loss of £24 million investment capital brought about a mini-crisis, as well as much unwelcome press publicity.*10 One consequence was a steep rise in local taxation which brought pressures for cutting local services.*11 Significantly, Gaelic education and cultural pursuits were not affected by post-BCCI economies.

It is significant that to date, Comhairle Nan Eilean is one of the few remaining non-party councils in Britain.*12 Although there exist active Hebridean Labour and Scottish National Party organisations, along with a small local Conservative association, their rivalries are restricted to parliamentary elections. Until 1994, local elections were

Pupils on their way to classes at Meanscoil, Beal Feirste

(courtesy of The Irish News)

Leitrim, Co. Down, is home to the oldes t GAA club in the county and boasted native Irish speakers until the 1930's.

(courtesy of The Irish News)

The Clydesdale Bank in Oban complete with the use of Gaelic. Official use of the language on civic and commercial buildings, and on road signs hasn't been an issue in Scotland, wheras in Northern Ireland it has been and still is a controversial issue.

Photo: David Alloway (CNG)

Street signs in Scottish Gaelic, this one in Inverness. But in Northern Ireland this has been a bone of contention for years...

(courtesy of CNG)

Bed and breakfast in Oban

(David Alloway CNG)

Gearoid O'Caireallain, Belfast-based President of Conradh na Gaeilge and founder/editor of La
(courtesy La)

Gearoid O'Cairerallain with GAA President Joe McDonagh

(courtesy of La)

Depopulation of Gaeltacht areas has been an ongoing problem in both Ireland and Scotland. The countryside in both countries is scattered with deserted farmhouses, such as this one in Clanvaraghan, Co Down. Irish was spoken in the area until 1895.

(Courtesy of Patrick O'Hare, Mourne Observer)

A cross marking the original site of the Franciscan Monastery in Drumnaquoile, Co . Down
(courtesy of Patrick O'Hare, Mourne Observer)

Patsy McGlone, SDLP councillor and gaeilgeoir
(courtesy of The Irish News)

Forbairt, Belfast's Gaelic Economic Forum was recently at the centre of controversy with the Northern Ireland Office over the use of Irish in official meetings

(courtesy of La)

John Robb pictured in Belfast

(courtesy of La)

Children being taught in the Gaelic medium in Ulster (La)

Meanscoil Feirste pupils pictured with vice primcipal Prionnsios O La Bhradha
(courtesy of La)

Gaelic revilalism in action...An Irish language college at Castlewellan, County Down
(courtesy of Patrick O'Hare, Mourne Observer)

Gaelic medium schoolchildren on the Isle of Lewis, Outer Hebrides
(courtesy of R. Huckbody, Stornoway Gazette)

Young musicians at the Ceolas Music School, part of the Gaelic Arts Project in Lewis
(courtesy of Rod Huckbody, Stornoway Gazette)

A Hebridean Choir at the 1994 Scottish National Mod, Dingwall. Courtesy of Rod Huckbody, Stornoway Gazette)

In full voice...Gaelic singing choir pictured in Stornoway practising for the National Mod in 1994
(Rod Huckbody, Stornoway Gazette)

Beautiful scenery is common to both Scotland and Ireland, but a good view is not enough to sustain a community. Slieveniskey was one of Down's last Gaeltachtai

(courtesy of Patrick O'Hare, Mourne Observer)

In many cases Irish learning classes started on a small scale, but now have undergone something of a popular revolution. This one is in Belfast

(courtesy of La)

Donald John Maciver

The 1997 Annual Congress of Comunn na Gaidhlig, Inverness.

Courtesy of Ewan Weatherspoon.

Joe McDonagh, GAA President, at a Glor na nGael presentation ceremony in Andersonstown Leisure Centre, West Belfast, in 1997.

(courtesy of La)

An early gathering of Coisde Gael Uladh

(courtesy of the Linenhall Library, Belfast)

The late Cardinal Tomas O'Fiaich

Young dancers at the Castlewellan Fleadh, Co Down, in 1994.
(Courtesy of Patrick O'Hare, Mourne Observer)

The late Donald Stewart MP, Scottish Nationalist member for the Western Isles, 1970-1987, who died in August 1992. Donald was sponsor of the 1981 Gaelic (Miscellaneous Provisions) Private Members Bill in the Commons, which was sadly unsuccessful.

Courtesy of Rod Huckbody, Stornoway Gazette.

St Kilda...home to the St Kilda Parliament, held in the house on the left in this 1886 picture. The body, consisting of the 100 per cent Gaelic-speaking island's adult males, met daily to discuss oppropriate communal tasks. St Kilda was evacuated in 1930.

(courtesy of ACG)

characterised by local issues and candidates fought on non-party slates. However, 1994 saw the election of four Labour Party candidates, the SNP declined to field official candidates. Yet even with Labour's 1994 initiative, plus Calum Macdonald's (Labour) successful challenges in 1992 and 1997, it looks unlikely that party politics will take over at the Comhairle. Clearly, Gaelic interests in the Western Isles have benefited from a mixture of lobbying by An Comunn Gaidhealach and the positive practices of Comhairle Nan Eilean. The Comhairle has shown itself to be an active sponsor of Gaelic interests and has been helped by the prevalence of Gaelic attitudes at the Scottish Office and among broadcasters and academics. It remains to be seen how those allies will withstand the effects of increasing Europeanisation over the next couple of decades. Their support is essential for Gaeldom's survival into the third millennium.

Elsewhere the Highlands Regional Council has also proved to be a staunch supporter of Gaelic interests. The Council, which came into existence in 1996 as part of a Scottish local government reform programme, has a policy commitment to upholding the status of Gaelic in education, the arts and general community affairs. It appointed a Gaelic education adviser, Dr Donald John Macleod, who was previously education director at Comunn na Gaidhlig, and who recently drafted a discussion paper on the future of Gaelic education throughout Scotland.*13

Interestingly, Highlands Council, like Comhairle Nan Eilean, is run by independents, though there are several pledged Liberal Democrats, Labour and Nationalist councillors, along with a small Tory force. The parliamentary seat of Ross, Skye and Inverness is held by Liberal Democrat Charles Kennedy, while fellow Liberals Ray Michie and Robert Maclennan hold the neighbouring Argyll and Bute and Caithness and Sutherland seats respectively. David Stewart (Labour) won Inverness, Nairm and Lochaber by a narrow majority in May 1997.

Highlands Council's catchment area includes the Isle of Skye, where the percentage of native Gaelic speakers amounts to some 60 per cent of local citizens. If this figure is added to that of the neighbouring Lochalsh, approximately 46 per cent of the districts population are native speakers. Accordingly, while demand for Gaelic educational and cultural facilities is not as great as it is on the Western Isles, it is still considerable. Unlike the Western Isles, Skye, Lochalsh and the entire Highlands region must cope with a substantial influx of affluent English speakers from the Lowlands and from England,. Most new incomers - nicknamed 'White Settlers' - hold little or no knowledge of Gaelic, and even less interest. Moreover it must be said that their presence and numbers stimulates inflation in the local housing market. thereby impairing "locals' in their capacity to acquire affordable housing. Such pressure compels many local people to go elsewhere, which has the effect of debilitating the local Gaelic population. Similar spectacles have been experienced by the native speaking communities in Wales, faced with a similar influx by droves of monoglot English second home buyers, largely from London and the so-called Home Counties.*14

It is self-evident from social and environmental factors how non-gaelic incomers have had an anglicising effect on the character of the area. Although the district contains a fair quota of bilingual road signs, and although there is a Radio na Gaidhlig studio in Portree, together with a council that helps local Gaelic organisations up to the limits of its budget, the fact is that Skye's Gaelic identity has been diluted by slow demographic changes. How far these trends will continue remains to be seen. Meanwhile, the safeguarding of existing crafts with grants and local preferences may act to retain the indigenous population, thus preserving the traditional Gaelic character of Skye. It is worth noting that Skye contains the only substantial Scottish Gaidhealtachd outside the Outer Hebrides. There is here a heritage factor that makes the preservation of its indigenous character essential.

The Gaelic medium education policy (see Chapter 5) operates on Skye with results that are mostly encouraging.*15 Perhaps of equal importance is the location of Sabhal Mor Ostaig on the island, which since its formation in 1972 has grown beyond the role of a mere Gaelic medium further Education college. Sabhal Mor Ostaig's status as a national Gaelic institution makes it something of a pillar in Scottish Gaeldom's slowly developing world. Its essence is tied up with being a redoubtable leader and pioneer in Gaelic vocational education, as well as a 'brains trust' for proposing Gaelic policy and future agendas. Accordingly for as long as the college retains leading status in the Gaelic world, Skye's Gaelic character looks assured. However the commercial anglicising trends have not been wholly stemmed, thus requiring that Gaeldom's defences be based on the solid and assorted foundations of Gaelic medium education, literature, arts and media. Anything less might not endure in the long term.

POLITICAL ACTION:

Political campaigns among Scottish Gaels have been few over recent years, with there being a preference instead for the lobbying activities of groups such as An Comunn Gaidhealach and Comunn na Gaidhlig

Evidence presented in this study shows how the Scottish Gaels avoided not just the nationalist embrace, as in Ireland, but also the radical image projected by Irish and Welsh language groups. Their interests had been furthered by wooing influential patrons in the Scottish media, churches, publishing, educational and arts worlds. This track record has generated a consensus for Gaelic interests across the party spectrum in Scotland, thereby ensuring a positive response from successive governments from the mid-1960's onwards. Accordingly there was less demand for an ongoing political campaign along Irish lines. Even the radical 1970's and 1980's movement, Comunn na Canain Albannaich, never proved more than marginal in its impact. With the Scottish Office showing an increasingly benign hand in funding education, arts and publishing, radical tactics thus seemed inappropriate to many leading figures in the Gaelic world.*16

This contemporary consensus was reflected in an ad-hoc Commons Gaelic Affairs Committee, whose membership included Calum Macdonald (Labour), Brian Wilson(Labour), Sir Russell Johnstone (Liberal Democrat), Ray Michie(Liberal Democrat), the late Sir Nicholas Fairburn (Conservative) and Bill Walker(Conservative).*17 By winning patrons across the party spectrum for their cause, Scottish Gaels ensured a continuity of public backing for their interests.

Yet for all its recent forward strides, Gaelic still lacks statutory recognition in Scotland. Moreover, the position of Gaelic as a medium of official and legal communications remains unclear, even in Gaidhealtachd areas. Donald Stewart's unsuccessful private member's bill of 1981 sought to rectify the gaps in statutory recognition, before falling prey to English Tory filibusters. It should also be added that the various gains for Gaelic have not stemmed the decline of native Gaelic speakers. Nor have An Comunn Gaidhealach or its sister bodies succeeded in halting the slow anglicisation of the Gailhealtachd in the Western Isles. Given the vast socio-economic advantages enjoyed by English as a medium of commerce and media communications, perhaps it is unrealistic to expect that Gaelic could compete, even in its own cradle territory. It remains to be seen how durable are the Gaidhealtachd communities in the twenty-first century, because it is they -rather than the second language gaels - who hold the key to the language's survival.

At the time of writing (July 1997) the new Labour Government of Prime Minister Tony Blair, and Scottish Secretary Donald Dewar, has announced a definite programme for the creation of a Scottish Parliament.*18 Given that the current Scottish Office Minister responsible for Gaelic Affairs is Brian Wilson (a Gaelic speaker), it would seem that Gaelic organisations are entitled to hope for a positive dialogue.*19 However, with the likelihood of devolved Home Rule occurring within the lifetime of the 1997 Parliament, Comunn na Gadhlig took the initiative. A conference was called for Spring 1997, papers produced and a campaign initiated for secure status for the Gaelic language and its various interests in Scotland. Moreover, their precise legal status to be accorded the language by the planned new Scottish Parliament has been of particular interest to CNG and its affiliated bodies.*20 In view of the positive policies of all mainstream Scottish Parties, there seems little danger of Gaelic reforms being reversed by a future Edinburgh administration. That said, CNG's role is to be a watchdog for Gaelic interests, and thus its secure status campaign is within its legitimate remit.

NORTHERN IRELAND: The progress of Gael Uladh continued at a slower pace than that of its Scottish counterpart, and was more limited in scope. It was also spread over a variety of initiatives and encountered fierce opposition from Unionist political foes.

The slow incorporation of Gaelic into the civic culture of Northern Ireland received a boost from the Anglo-Irish Agreement.*21 The Agreement - co-signed by the London and dublin Governments - specifically pledged to "...foster the cultural heritage of both traditions...and...the avoidance of economic and social discrimination..."*22. Earlier articles had specified respect for the two political identities, with obvious benefits for the language and culture of the Nationalist Minority.*16 Moreover, the creation of a joint conference that included the Republic's representatives for monitoring the treaty provisions, ensured that Irish culture had an influential sponsor. Accordingly, from the 1985 Hillsborough accord followed a period of gradual inclusion for the Gaelic language, sport and culture, with public funding and other entitlements accruing on a scale hitherto unknown in the Six Counties.

One key area of advancement has occurred in broadcasting. Some Irish language programmes have appeared on BBC Northern Ireland and independent TV and radio, while an irish language unit has opened at Radio Foyle, Derry. Additionally, the coverage of Gaelic sports, especially performances of premier Ulster Gaelic Footballing counties such as Down, Tyrone, Derry and Donegal, along with Antrim and Down hurlers, has increased to mainstream levels. Such has been prompted partly by a new spirit of cultural pluralism, but also by the recent success of those counties in All-Ireland premier competitions.*23 However, as Maguire noted, there are no scheduled Gaelic language programmes, nor has BBC Northern Ireland or Ulster Television taken a lead in encouraging new initiatives in that area.*24 Nothing along the lines of Scottish television's 'Machair' soap either appears or is planned by the broadcasters of Northern Ireland, nor has there been any irish language learner programmes similar to BBC Scotland's 'Can Seo' series. Evidently the practice of Northern Irish broadcasters has been to react rather than initiate. Moreover, developments occurring in respect of the Gaelic language, sports and cultural broadcasts have taken place against regular Unionist protests. The latter have been couched in emotive phrases, suggesting that Gaelic broadcasts are akin to undermining the"British" and "Protestant" ways of life. Also, Unionist objectors frequently cite connections between gaelic cultural aims and the republican political agenda*25 and make the most of the GAA's disputatious rule 21.*26 While the protests may appear shrill, it is important to recall that less than thirty years ago similar prejudices prevailing at the top of the BBC were used to keep Gaelic-Irish culture off-screen in Northern ireland,. In that sense, changing times have meant changing policy.

The hillsborough spirit of cultural pluralism has extended to community arts funding. Northern Ireland's Arts Council has over the past ten years slowly increased its funding for Gaelic drama and related initiatives. Additionally, 1989 saw the creation of ULTACHT Trust. This body is aided as part of the Cultural Traditions Group of the Northern Ireland Community Relations Council, and its sponsorship owes something to the Northern Ireland Office's desire to see the Irish language and culture to be promoted beyond traditional nationalist bounds. The Trust - whose trustees have included nationalists like former GAA president, Peter Quinn, and ex-Unionist Party General Secretary, Cllr Chris McGimpsey - has responsibility for distributing awards from its annual budget to voluntary language groups, as well as assisting in publishing ventures.

Funding comes from three main sources. The original Northern Ireland Office grant of £65,000 (*27) was increased to £90,000 (1996-7) and is augmented by a grant from the Republic's Government of IR£20,000. A capital fund generates additional income of £85,000 per annum. After covering salaries and office costs, the Trust distributed £100,000 in grants to Irish language groups and causes over 1996 and 1997. *28

Since the mid-1970s Northern Ireland Office grant aid to the GAA has also increased. In 1977, the publicly funded Ulster Sports Council appointed a full-time Hurling Developments Officer. Later, other Gaelic coaching and development positions were created to the point that now the GAA in each of the Six Counties compete for youth and cultural project funding. Additionally, as considered in Chapter Five, there has been a steady growth in the numbers of Irish medium educational units. Indeed the Buncsoileanna and Irish Playschool movement ranks as Northern Ireland's fastest growing educational sector, but until recently received little or no state funding.

The political significance of these developments is that Ulster Gaeldom in its language, cultural and sporting dimensions is gradually being accommodated by the civic culture of Northern Irish society.

However, such gains have not been trouble free, nor have they caused Gaelic associations to weaken their relationship with political nationalism. The pace of change has not satisfied everyone, as will be shown later.

WEST BELFAST GAELTACHT: The pilot Gaeltacht at Paric Ros Goill, Shaws Road, and described so comprehensively in Dr Maguire's book, has been enlarged by new developments.

Although Shaw's Road families now number sixteen, in fact a wider community of Irish speaking households mushroomed in the city throughout the 1980's. This community now generates such services as Gaelic nursery and primary schools, literature, arts, music and an economic network. Hence there has evolved in West Belfast's Gaeltacht an embryo social infra-structure.

La's emergence as Ireland's leading Irish language paper stimulated other initiatives in West Belfast's Gaeilgeoir community. Additional to a growing Bunscoileanna movement, an Irish arts centre grew up on the Falls Road. By 1997, this centre, named Culturlann Macadam/O'Fiaich, (in memory of the 19th century Belfast Presbyterian Gaeilgeoir Robert Macadam and the late Cardinal and Gaelic scholar Cardinal Tomas O'Fiaich) accommodated various enterprises.

These included La's offices, Meanscoil Feirste (Belfast Irish medium secondary school), an Irish book store, a shop, cafe and Gaelic theatre and recording studio. *29 It is significant that all those services operate on a commercial basis, and grew up in response to demand from local Gaeilgeoiri and the wider Nationalist community of Belfast.

The organisation and funding of the Culturlann highlights the Northern Ireland Office's post-Anglo Irish Agreement inclusiveness policy. Its premises are leased from a Catholic diocesan agency, Springfield Association, but the £20,000 annual rent has been wholly met by the Northern Ireland Department of the Environment since 1991. The 'tenant' organisations contained within, meet their own running costs and pay rent to the Culturlann itself. The DOE grant runs out this year (1997) and Culturlann's management committee are seeking alternative funding from the Northern Ireland Arts Council. *30 The track record of the latter gives good grounds to believe that the application will be successful.

The experiences of La show an intermittent dependence on various public funding sources, albeit with a capacity for survival in hard times. La's long standing founding editor Gearoid O'Caireallain, an ardent Republican, has nevertheless maintained the paper's independence from both the SDLP and Sinn Fein. *32 The paper is run under the direction of its editor, and overseen by a broad-based board of directors. (For details see Appendix 4). However, that did not spare the paper a British Government accusation of being a front for Sinn Fein, in 1989. After moving around different locations between 1986 and 1988, La operated from the old Conway Mill in the Lower Falls, sharing the premises with the Irish action group Glor na nGael. When the latter's funds were suspended in 1989, by directive of the then NIO Minister Brian Mawhinney, La also lost its grant. Mawhinney argued that the Conway Mill was a centre of IRA sponsored activity and declared it to be out of bounds for public funding. Interestingly he never produced evidence of this beyond "intelligence reports."

Also, Glor na Gael's plight was taken up by a wide range of Nationalist groups including the SDLP, Sinn Fein and the Irish Government. Funding was eventually restored in 1991, by which time La had moved to its current address. *33 Since then its relationship with the Northern Ireland Office has been one of uneasy cordiality.

The paper operates as a small business, with a combined staff of six, including editorial and advertising staff as well as a commercial manager. Revenue comes from a variety of sources, including sales and advertising, and subsidies - which include an NIO grant in kind for computer equipment and a smaller sum from Bord na Gaeilge, the Republic's statutory Irish language council. An ACE grant from the Northern Ireland DOE enabled La to hire a temporary official - creating subsequent ACE posts - during 1993/4. *34

In January 1994 the paper was selling 1,000 copies per week, 500 by subscription in Dublin, 300 in Belfast and the rest in various locations around the country. Significantly it has had a greater appeal among second language Gaels, and sells very little in Gaeltacht areas. *35 La has also in the past faced competition from Anois, the Dublin-based Gael Linn paper, which until 1995 was subsidised by the Irish Government. Loss of funding forced its closure, allowing La to pick up many of the former Anois readers.

By July 1997, despite the launch of another Irish Government sponsored paper, Galway-based Foinse, La had a weekly circulation of 4,000. Almost half of the total are sold in the Six Counties, with 800 per week in Belfast alone. The largest point of sale outside the North is Dublin. *36 La's position has never been healthier and Gearoid O'Caireallain views the future positively:

*"La and the Culturlann provide a community function for the Irish speaking people of West Belfast and further afield. The paper gives literary impetus to the Gaeilgeoiri vision of a parallel society in the Six Counties; one in which the services of the state and its infrastructure are provided within the medium of Irish." *37*

Nor is that 'parallel society' vision confined to La or Gaelic medium education, for it has slowly made in-roads to vocational and economic areas. Several local employment and business initiatives are currently under way among Belfast's Irish speakers, the most prominent being Forbairt Feirste. Created in 1995 as an economic agency, and modelled on the Welsh group Menter-Y-Busness, it seeks to identify positive employment prospects for Irish speakers.

Forbairt, funded by the Northern Ireland Training and Employment Agency, has set up two Irish medium training courses; one in Media Studies, the other in Business Administration. The aim is to prepare Belfast's Irish speakers for running their own businesses and there are firm plans to develop a technical sector at the Meanscoil. *38

Assessment of Belfast's Gaeilgeoir community must consider two further factors. One is the rising esteem of that community, while the other concerns the role of political Nationalists.

Undoubtedly the success of Belfast Gaeilgeoiri has been generated by a sustained programme involving the laying of structural foundations for the 'parallel society.' The various Irish medium educational initiatives along with city-wide language classes, La, Shaws Road Gaeltacht, the Culturlann and embryo economic structures, have all contributed to a distinctive and viable community.

That community is currently developing further structures, such as may sustain the socio-infrastructure and economic roots, guaranteeing long term viability.

Indicative of the rising esteem is the fact that Gearoid O'Caireallain was elected, in 1995, as National President of Conradh na Gaeilge, a position he currently holds on a semi-full time basis, and for which he has taken temporary leave from La. The holding of the 1997 Oireachtas (arts festival) in Belfast has further boosted Gaeilgeoiri pride in the city.

But the political environment of West Belfast is of prime relevance to the Gaeilgeoir community's advancement. There are four sources of political influence: two being statutory and the other two being political parties.

First is the Northern Ireland Office, whose attitude has been one of grudging acquiesence and cautious assistance. Second is Belfast City Council, whose Unionist majority maintained a hostile position until the early 1990s. One former Lord Mayor, the DUP's Sammy Wilson, once infamously described Irish as a "leprechaun language." In the Northern Ireland local elections of 1997, Unionists lost control of the City Council for the first time ever, falling to a loose coalition of SDLP, Alliance and Sinn Fein representatives. And the city gained its first Nationalist Lord Mayor in the SDLP's Alban Maguinness, a Belfast barrister. *39 His agenda prioritises an 'inclusive' policy for both political traditions, with the Irish language to be accorded due parity of esteem alongside other cultures. *40

The resumed IRA ceasefire (July 20, 1997) holds out the prospect of a substantial peace dividend, in terms of further grants and entitlements for the Irish language. This potential, while lucrative, is still uncertain amidst the fluid state of political developments.

The influence of Sinn Fein in Belfast's Gaeilgeoir movement is one constantly emphasised by Unionist opponents, who see Irish and its support as an appendix to Republicanism. In fact the reality is rather different. Gaelic culture, sports and the Irish language, as noted by the Opshal Commission, are an integral part of the cultural life of the Nationalist people of the Six Counties. *41 Predictably, culture and political identity fuse to assume special status in the adverse conditions affecting Nationalists through partition and the Unionist ascendancy. Yet the culture being an indigenous part of Nationalist community life is hardly the product of machinations by any party or its activists. Put simply, Gaeilgeoirism, Gaelic sports and music were always there. Those seeking to Sinn Fein for the building of Belast's Gaeilgeoir community reveal a grave misunderstanding of Northern Nationalist life.

Sinn Fein and the SDLP have both staunchly pro-Gaeilgeoir policies. Several activists from both parties have taken leading roles in related organisations, with Sinn Feiners being more active in West Belfast and the SDLP in rural areas.

The former Belfast Sinn Fein councillor Mairtin O'Muilleoir has written articles for La, as well as being a former chairman of Glor na nGael. And a majority of Sinn Fein councillors and party workers, along with the party's two MPs Gerry Adams and Martin McGuinness, are Irish speakers. The party publishes documents and press releases in both languages, holds meetings in Irish and actively backs the Bunscoileanna, La, Culturlann and other Gaelic groups.

The SDLP likewise priorities the language, as demonstrated in its 19864 policy document co-authored by the party's former General Secretary and current Cookstown councillor and talks delegate Patsy McGlone, and Mourne councillor Hugh Carr. *42

The SDLP has made the running for Irish language recognition in several local councils and has a bilingual medium policy for conducting its business. However it lacks a substantial presence in West Belfast; where its membership is thin, councillors are fewer than those of Sinn Fein, and former MP Dr Joe Hendron lost his seat to Gerry Adams. *43

Gearoid O'Caireallain readily acknowledges the commitment of both Nationalist parties to the language, while noting the fact of Sinn Fein's dominance in the West Belfast community:

"Sinn Fein prioritises the Irish language, whereas the SDLP contains committed individuals; and because of those individuals the party has been a supporter of language projects.....In West Belfast, Sinn Fein are a genuine community action organisation with roots in most areas of community life. This gives the party (SF) an advantage in effecting its Gaeilgeoir policies." *44

<u>NEWRY AND MOURNE COUNCIL:</u> There has been a novel bilingual experiment at Newry and Mourne Council in County Down; itself partly symbolic and part-utilitarian. Predictably the Gaelic language experiment owes its purpose to the Council's Nationalist character - the SDLP forms the largest political bloc - which reflects the nature of the wider area.

Newry and Mourne is unable to replicate the bilingual programme of Comhairle Nan Eilean, for two reasons. Firstly, although the Gaelic language enjoys an active legacy throughout South Down and South Armagh, in fact it is over sixty years since the last native speakers died. Unlike the Outer Hebrides, Newry and Mourne has no traditional Gaeltacht; hence the case for Gaelic medium education and services has a cultural, but not utilitarian, basis. Second, there is the practical reality that Newry, like other Northern Ireland councils, has no control over education, housing or social services. Those services are managed by Area Boards and the Northern Ireland Housing Executive, to which councils nominate members.

There is not the capacity for mounting a major bilingual campaign, thereby leaving the Council to utilise its limited functions of tourism, refuse collection, environment and planning. The Council's policy is to promote the Irish language as a cultural option, and an avenue for popular understanding of the area's folk heritage.

This Gaelic experiment began in 1986 with the establishment of an Irish language sub-committee, Coiste na Gaeilge, as an advisory forum to the Council's Recreation and Tourist Committee. In

January, 1990, it adopted an official bilingual name, with bilingual symbols, shield and selective notices. It pledged support for local Gaelic cultural and educational projects, and has since twinned with Comhairle Nan Eilean and Clare County Council. An official calendar featuring the logo of all three councils has been produced as a result. *45

There is also a Council-sponsored Gaelic arts programme, that includes Irish language classes. The post of Irish Language Development Officer was created in 1987. Its first and long running encumbent, Maolcholaim Scott, had a track record of Gaeilgeoir writing, research and community initiatives, and over his time encouraged further developments. The latter included preparations for a local Bunscoil (then struggling without Government aid) and setting up a local Gaelic printing company, Clo Ruari Community Business Teo, established on a non profit basis to assist local Irish voluntary groups. *46

Generally Newry and Mourne Council's language campaign has made headway, despite restraints. The Newry experience has prompted other councils, including Down, Derry and Dungannon to start comparable initiatives, but none has yet adopted a full bilingual policy.

It is noteworthy that in Newry the traditional Unionist hostility has been relaxed, as the involvement of Protestant Gaels from both Ulster and Scotland becomes more apparent. Maolcholaim Scott's own background (he is the son of a Lisburn Presbyterian Minister) played no small part in the wooing process. Unionist councillors have taken part in twinning visits to the Hebrides, which appears to suggest a willingness to re-appraise former taboos. Perhaps some Unionists are now ready to re-analyse their Gaelic heritage, most being descended from Scotland.

However it remains to be seen how far such cultural revisionism will proceed, especially in the Loyalist hinterlands of Down, Antrim and the Lagan Valley.

Political Assessments: Despite the rising fortunes of Ulster Gaeilgeoiri there remains a lingering suspicion among Gael Uladh that institutional hostility is still intact in the Unionist and British establishment. This has been fuelled by the underfunding of Bunscoileanna and the Glor na nGael affair.

Pol O'Muiri had this to say of Glor na nGael's experience:

*"Not surprisingly with a track record like this, Irish speakers do not hold the authorities in very great esteem. Their hostility towards the language fluctuates from being hostile to patronising to obstructive. The policy seems to be, to do as little as possible whenever possible, and when backed into a corner, to spend money on academic projects which, while worthwhile, do little to alleviate the daily struggle of so many other schemes." *47*

A similar viewpoint on NIO prejudices comes from Maolcholaim Scott:

*"...no organ of Government recognises a right to choice in use of the language. In practice, most, and this includes the majority of local authorities, prefer to exclude Irish Gaelic from their arts and heritage programmes, arguing that it does not have a 'consensus' or 'across the board support.' Few arts or heritage projects do, and this is an illustration that, if Irish is politicised, that various branches of Government and state-funded institutions are part and parcel of this; no language can be de-politicised, English least of all; what can be done is to ensure a broader range of participations." *48*

The 1991 NIO Census recorded 142,003 persons as having some knowledge of Irish Gaelic, with a further 70,000 acknowledged as holding oral and literate fluency. *49 This figure represents a high proportion of the total number of Celtic language speakers - Scottish Gaelic, Irish Gaelic and Welsh - which the UK census totalled at 725,000. *50

Gael Uladh have long complained of being underfunded in comparison to the treatment afforded to Scottish Gaels and have some justification in doing so.

Aid to Irish groups totalled £1,276,000 in 1991/2, compared to £12,000,000 for their Scottish counterparts.

The last word lies with SDLP councillor Patsy McGlone, who sums it all up:

"The British Government attempts to give the appearance of being well disposed towards the language. Yet most of the projects have flourished entirely as a consequence of the commitment and effort of community-based organisations to see them succeed, and usually in spite of Government policy. The glaring truth is that these figures show a seriously discriminatory approach to the Irish language by the British Government. It is high time....that the Irish language is placed on an equal footing with Scottish Gaelic and Welsh." *51

The disparity in funding, access and policies of the Government, visa-viz the two national Gaelic communities, holds fundamental ramifications for the future of both lobbies.

FOOTNOTES AND REFERENCES:

1. *Croft Recordings, Western Isles, Scotland, 1990.*
2. *Aberdeen Press and Journal, Oban Times, West Highland Free Press, Stornoway Gazette.*

3. Hunter (1976)

4. Comhairle Nan Eilean, 1986.

5. Ibid., p.1

6. Correspondence V.McKee and Dolina McLeod 1990/1

7. McKee (1995) Contemporary Politics p.99

8. Eirigh agus Soirbherachadh nam Meadhanan Gaidhlig, May 1996

9. Contemporary Politics, Municipal Journal 1995 and 1991.

10. Municipal Journal, July 19, 1991.

11.(i) As a result of the BCCI losses incurred in June 1991, the Council Finance Director, Donald Macleod, was dismissed.The Chief Executive, Dr George Macleod, was initially dismissed, but reinstated on appeal; he was allowed to take early retirement in1992.Rev. Donald Macauley, Council Convenor, resigned in Autumn 1991, amidst accusations of "weak leadership" during the BCCI crisis. (ii) Gaelic medium was not affected by the Comhairle's post-BCCI economies, as it was funded directly from the Scottish Office's Specific Grants for Gaelic Medium Education.

12.Richard Parry Scottish Political Facts, (1989, Edinburgh)

13.'Framework for Growth: A National Policy for Gaelic Education' Comunn na Gaidhlig, 1997.- Prepared by Gaelic Education Action Group;members listed in Appendix 6.

14. Peter Berrseford Ellis The Celtic Revolution, Chap 4, Wales, pp. 94-97. (1985, Ceridigion, Wales).

15. In 1996, Skye had a total of five Gaelic Medium Primary School units, with a total of 222 pupils.A Gaelic Medium Secondary unit exists at Portree Secondary School, with a total of 17 pupils (1996), and also a Gaelic Medium Nursery Unit with 18 pupils. Ref. Correspondance from Donald John Maciver/V McKee Comhairle Nan Eilean Gaelic Education section, 2nd July 1997.

Note A full list of Gaelic Medium units shall be listed in Appendix 5.

16.The preference for lobbying and working with various local government and Scottish Office authorities, as opposed to radical protests which expressed by almost all leading figures in the Scottish Gaelic world, with whom this author spoke.

17. McKee, (1995), Contemporary Politics pp 98-99

18. Green paper on the future devolved Scottish Parliament; HMSO, July 24, 1997, London and Edinburgh.

19. Brian Wilson has long been associated with The West Highland Free Press for whom he was regular weekly columnist. He is a Gaelic speaker, has family connections with Lewis, and contested (unsuccessfully) the Western Isles seat against the late Donald Stewart, at the 1983 general election. Wilson was subsequently elected in 1987 to represent another Scottish constituency at Westminster and following Labour's victory in May 1997, he was appointed as Scottish Office Minister with special responsibility for Gaelic affairs.

20. See Congress Report of CNG campaign for Secure Status for Gaelic, CNG Inverness June 1997.

21. Anglo Irish Agreement, November 1985, HMSO.

22. Anglo Irish Agreement, article 5a.

23. Jerome Quinn, Ulster Gaelic Games Annual 1994

24. Maguire, 1991 Chapter 4. pp 57-59.

25. During the 70s and 80s various Northern Ireland councils refused grant aid to GAA clubs and MPs including Ian Paisley accused the Association of having Republican links.

26. i Rule 21, Official Guide, GAA: "Members of the British armed forces shall not be eligible for membership of the Association. A member of the Association participating in dances or similar entertainment promoted by, or under the patronage of such bodies, shall incur suspension of at least three months."

ii. There has been a concerted move by sections of the Association to be rid of Rule 21. In 1978 London GAA sought to have it repealed, and a more comprehensive effort was attempted in 1995 at the GAA's annual congress. Meanwhile Warwickshire GAA ignores the rule and has members of the police among players, referees and officials.

27. McKee, Contemporary Politics, 1995 p102

28. Communique A. MacPoilin (director, Ultacht Trust) to Patsy McGlone, July 9, 1997.

29. McKee, Contemporary Politics, 1995, p. 106 and interviews with Gearoid O'Caireallain July 1994 and 1997.

30. Ibid

31. Ibid

32. La has published contributions from prominent figures in the SDLP and Sinn Fein. The paper's appeal is partly its independence from party manipulations.

33. Interviews with Gearoid O'Caireallain, January and July 1994.

34. Ibid

35. Ibid

36. Ibid

37. Interview with Gearoid O'Caireallain, January 1994.

38. as above, in July 1997.

39. Irish News, May 30, 1997.

40. Ibid

41. Torkel Opsahl, A Citizen's Inquiry: The Opsahl Report on Northern Ireland, Dublin 1993.

42. Caipeis Pholosai na Gaeilge/Irish Language Policy Paper, SDLP 1986.

43. SDLP organisation in West Belfast is thin - Sinn Fein is stronger by far.

44. Interview Gearoid O'Caireallain July 21, 1997.

45. McKee, 1991, Municipal Journal.

46. Correspondence Maolcholaim Scott to McKee, October 28, 1993.

47. Pol O'Muiri The Irish Review - An Ghaelige (Belfast 1993).

48. Letter, Maolcholaim Scott to McKee, October 1, 1990.

49. Northern Ireland Census 1991. HMSO Belfast 1992, p.159.

50. British Census 1991.

51. Patsy McGlone press briefing, December 21, 1993; also Irish News, December 22, 1993.

CHAPTER 5
GAELIC MEDIUM EDUCATION IN SCOTLAND & NORTHERN IRELAND

So far, this study has focussed on the historic and contemporary evolution of Gaelic in both countries, inclusive of its decline and mini-resurgence. Chapter 4 provides an appraisal of Gaelic in the communities of Scotland and Northern Ireland, taking special account of the new structures that had emerged over the preceding decades in both countries. This chapter shall be concerned with the special part played by education in the resurgence, most particularly Gaelic medium education. The latter has taken firm root - albeit in different forms - in the two countries. So too has it come to symbolise the language's best hope for long term survival among current and future generations.

In their respective accounts, Kenneth MacKinnon and Gabrielle Maguire have each alluded - albeit sympathetically - to the low status hurdle confronting Gaelic culture and the language in both countries. Essentially a lack of Gaelic literature and teaching materials has meant the language occupying a low position on the social ladder. Also as outlined in Chapters 1&2, historic suppression of Gaelic meant that by the twentieth century the educational systems of Scotland and Ireland, including Northern Ireland after partition, had been thoroughly anglicised, to the point that Gaelic was portrayed as an unrefined anachronism

.Therefore, aside from the political hostility of unionists and anglophiles, there was the fundamental difficulty of recasting the language as a worthwhile medium for educational instruction. Moreover, as Reg Hindley's 1990 study noted, this same status problem afflicted Southern Irish governments over successive decades in their endeavours to construct a Gaeilgeoir educational policy.*1

Even Gaeltacht dwellers showed a reluctance to accept the equal esteem of their language, alongside the commercial and international strength of English. As MacKinnon and Hindley each observed, there powerful institutional and commercial forces waging war against Gaelic, even in its poor and rural cradle territories of the Outer Hebrides, Skye, Donegal, Omeath, Connemara and Munster.*2

Thus a new initiative was required for restoring parity of esteem for Gaelic in the educational world. The latter was essential if language and culture were to have a viable future beyond the current generation.

Gaelic medium education was a practical means of laying durable foundations for the language. By providing instruction in all subjects through the medium of Gaelic (in secondary schools this was in most subjects, but subject to the availability of teachers) the link between home and community is maintained, which Gaeilgeoir educationalists insist is vital to the practical survival of Gaelic within and beyond the Gaeltacht/Gaidhealtachd.

Despite hostility from various quarters, political and establishment, in fact there is no evidence of linguistic defects nor stilted intellectual development in either country.

Indeed, the opposite effects have been more noticeable. Scottish and Irish Gaelic medium pupils join other nations, ie Belgium, Quebec, Malaysia, Phillipines and India, where bi/multilingual learning is central to basic curriculum development. Successive studies have confirmed this.

A 1987 report commissioned by the Scottish Office, undertaken by Stirling University, and focussed on the Western Isles, contained a positive appraisal of Hebridean bilingual education. *3 The report found that the Western Isles Bilingual Education Project, initiated in 1976, had been effective through being accepted and implemented by schools.

It also found bilingual teaching to be well established across the curriculum, with further developments sought. Another study

(1989) by Gaelic educationalist Dr Anne Lorne Gillies - recently turned SNP politician *4 found evidence of a welcome growth in positive attitudes to Gaelic medium/bilingual education among the wider Scottish population. *5 In her comprehensive study of the Belfast Gaeilgeoir community, Gabrielle Maguire noted that the unrelenting efforts of parents and a sympathetic Nationalist population had imbued Bunscoileanna children with a self-confidence resulting from decades of struggle and self-sacrifice that characterised West Belfast's nua-Gaeltacht. *6

So did Maguire's study find evidence of literary enhancement among Belfast and Derry Irish medium pupils, something which critics have been slow to acknowledge. *7

As this book is essentially a political scientist's evaluation of the various areas of Scottish and Ulster Gaeldom, it is thus inappropriate to trespass upon the educationalist's domain. However, in so far as Gaelic medium education has contributed to the political community of Gaeldom, it's workings and relationship with government are a legitimate area for inquiry. Hence there is value in looking more closely at the Gaelic medium schools and units (within schools) in both countries.

SCOTLAND: Scottish Gaelic medium education began in the Western Isles in 1986. It followed on from an earlier bilingual project, initiated by Comhairle Nan Eilean shortly after its inception in 1975.

Essentially, Gaelic medium education was a programme aimed at protecting the long term esteem and usage of the language by ensuring its place in the Scottish educational system. It involved an immersion in Gaelic for pupils through both academic instruction and socio-cultural activities. This process would ideally begin at play-school, follow on through primary school and lead into the secondary school stage.

It required Scottish Office funding for books, learning materials, trained teachers, a high degree of co-ordination and community support. Although pioneered in the Western Isles, it was always envisaged that Gaelic medium education would be extended elsewhere in the Highlands, Strathclyde and wherever else a parental demand existed. *8 The matter of parental initiative is central to the workings of the Gaelic medium education system. Gaelic medium units can only be established where there is parental demand, and children may be recruited only with parental consent.

In its workings, Gaelic medium education is pursued by way of units co-existing alongside mainstream classes in English medium schools. The latter schools, while providing substantial Gaelic language teaching and related cultural pursuits, teach through the medium of English. Gaelic medium units are aimed at pupils for whom Gaelic is the normal language in the home, which normally, but not exclusively, means the families of the Gaidhealtachd. It also embraces the children of dedicated second language Gaels in urban areas like Glasgow and Inverness. Such children learn English to high fluency level, but, significantly, as a second language, with all the cultural connotations that dimension entails.

Western Isles: Given the pioneering role played by Comhairle Nan Eilean, a key element in this initiative was the creation of the office of Bilingual Education Policy Advisor. This officer would have responsibility for leading the drive towards Gaelic medium development throughout the Outer Hebrides.

The person appointed was an eminent Scottish Gael, Donald John Maciver, a Gaelic author, with some seventeen titles to his distinction, and former Head of Gaelic Studies at the Nicholson Institute, Stornoway.

Additionally he was National President of An Comunn Gaidhealach for five years during the 1980's, has had a long association with various Gaelic cultural bodies all over Scotland. Such expert credentials were essential for ensuring the success of the Comhairle's campaign to persuade Islanders, especially parents and teachers, of the usefulness and viability of the Gaelic medium units within primary and junior secondary schools across the Outer Hebrides. The essence of winning parental support cannot be overstated, because the Gaelic medium units were parent-driven.

One of Maciver's main tasks in the early days concerned the persuasion of parents and the provision of confidence-building measures.

Furthermore, the same officer had to ensure that there were sufficient numbers of trained teachers, as well as monitoring newly formed units, planning additional ones and liaising with council and Scottish Office officials to structure the available finance and resources. *9

Spearheading the Western Isles Gaelic medium education programme was a formidable task, but then Maciver is a formidable man and his status, ability, drive and confidence left no one in doubt that the project was in good hands.

Results in the Outer Hebrides have been encouraging. Since its introduction in 1986, Gaelic medium units have been established in 24 primary schools, catering for 538 pupils (1996 figures). *10 This figure covers approximately 37 per cent of the total number of Gaelic medium unit (primary level) pupils throughout Scotland, who numbered 824 in 1993, rising to 1,456 in 1996. *11

Additionally, the Western Isles' first secondary Gaelic medium unit opened in 1993 at the Nicholson Institute in Stornoway, with other units following at Lionel Junior Secondary School, Ness, and Shawbost J.S. School, all on the Isle of Lewis. A further unit was scheduled to open at Sgoil Lionacleit, Benbecula, in September 1997.

It is anticipated that the new Castlebay Secondary School, Barra, will soon be receiving enough Gaelic medium pupils from its feeder primary schools to justify a unit of its own. *12

By September 1996, combined secondary Gaelic medium pupil numbers had reached 47, representing 36 per cent of the total Scottish Secondary Schools Gaelic medium population of 132. *13

The Comhairle's Bilingual Implementation Review envisages the Gaelic Medium Units developing from their current novel status into a comprehensive entity in the foreseeable future. *14 Parental demand is growing, and under Donald John Maciver's leadership, these units have been sustained through the difficult stages.

Considering the substantial grounding which even English medium pupils receive in Gaelic, the overall effect has been to ensure that the Hebridean children receive a substantial amount of their education in both languages and within the broad Gaelic culture.

Accordingly, a mixture of bilingualism and Gaelic medium education has further ensured that these children receive a positive image of their own Gaelic heritage. Such benefits were not so readily available to their parents' or grandparents' generations.

Elsewhere throughout the Highlands, Grampian and Strathclyde, the picture has been one of steady growth. Gaelic medium education has been making strides throughout the country, with particular progress in those areas boasting wither a Gaidhealtachd or Gaelic heritage. Appendix 5 shows the 1996 figures for Gaelic medium primary units, of which a breakdown of each local authority lists sixteen Highlands Regional Council units, five in the Strathclyde area, two in Grampian, two in Tayside and one in Edinburgh.

Secondary sector Gaelic medium figures - additional to the three existing Hebridean institutions - show three units in Strathclyde and four in the Highlands.

The growth in Gaelic medium units and Gaelic education generally has stimulated a demand for trained teachers. In particular, there has been an urgent demand for in-service training courses for Gaelic medium teachers from the colleges of education. Hence the Scottish Office has been lobbied by groups like Comunn Na Gaidhlig, An Comunn Gaidhealach and those local authorities offering substantial Gaelic education programmes, eg, Comhairle Nan Eilean and Highlands, for funds and access to suitable personnel to the new enabling requirements.

Another area of vital development in Gaelic medium education throughout Scotland has been the Gaelic Pre-School Groups. The essence of this service lies in its capacity to cater for the children of Gaelic speaking homes, both within and beyond the Gaidhealtachd, to initiate the educational process at the earliest stage of child development. Significantly, it is the Gaelic Playgroups who 'feed' Gaelic Medium Primary School units, and thus provide the core basis for subsequent progress of Gaelic children. Hence experiments in Gaelic Medium education have by necessity commenced in pre-school groups, linked to the community and operating with firm parental backing.

Appendix 6 contains full details of the Gaelic Playgroups.In July 1997, there were some 75 Gaelic Pre-School Groups throughout Scotland, which are all voluntary, albeit receiving the services of appropriately trained Nursery teachers, and with variable amounts of public aid.From latter figures, the following local authority area breakdown applies for individual groups: Western Isles 29, Highlands 27, Strathclyde 8, Aberdeen 4, Lothians 2, Dunblane 1, Perth & Kinross 4. * 15

Additionally, there are four local education authority Gaelic Nursery Schools; two in the Highlands and one each in the Western Isles and Lothians areas respectively. Those figures reaffirm the Western Isle's position as Scotland's principal Gaidhealtachd, with the greatest demand for Gaelic education at all levels.At the same time, the rising numbers of Gaelic Playgroups functioning outside traditional Gaidhealtachd areas, in places like Peterhead, Dunfermline, Perth, Edinburgh and Glasgow suggests that Gaelic education is acquiring a genuinely national appeal. Indeed the 2,500 Gaelic nursery pupils and their groups might be said to constitute Gaeldom's 'green shoots', whose vitality augers well for pupil-uptake of Gaelic medium education at subsequent levels over future years. Interestingly too, the scope of Gaelic Medium Playgroups has extended outside Scotland to ex-patriate Gaels. Presently(July 1997) there are Gaelic Nursery groups in London, Cape Breton and the Isle of Man. * 16

The Gaelic Playgroups are managed by an Inverness-based organisation, Comhairle Nan Sgoiltean Araich. Founded in 1983, this body has over its short lifetime experienced a vast increase in scope and funding, and has now become a major party in the

Scottish Gaelic education lobby.It enjoys some 96% grant aid from a mixture of Scottish Office, local enterprise and local authority sources.The balance comes in donations from voluntary benefactors. This reliable income enables the organisation to employ an energetic field officer, Fionnlagh M. Macleoid, along with a professional Secretary, Keith Scammell.* 17

It is because of stability of organisation and purpose that Comhairle Nan Sgoiltean Araich had developed swiftly and effectively, thereby enabling it to service ever-rising numbers of groups, in line with the growing demand for Gaelic medium pre-school education throughout Scotland and beyond.

OVERVIEW: The general picture of Scottish Gaelic Medium education is one of growth and consolidation. Although major pioneering initiatives are focussed on the Western Isles, there have been developments elsewhere in Scotland.

The emergence of a vibrant Gaelic Medium Nursery and Primary school sector, along with a developing Secondary sector, augers well for the language's future in Scottish education. While a majority of units are concentrated in Gaeldom's traditional kernel of the Highlands and Hebrides, the emergence of Gaelic Medium streams in Glasgow, Edinburgh, Dundee, Perth and Aberdeen underlines the language's widening appeal. Education is one of several arenas by which Gaeldom is gradually shedding its regional image in favour of a genuinely national one. How far this growth shall continue, and whether the Gaelic medium units will require fresh direction as a result of these changes, remains to be seen? Also, there is the matter of how a new Scottish Parliament will view Gaelic Medium education in terms of expenditure and policy. To that end, The Campaign for Secure Status for Gaelic - recently initiated by Comunn Na Gaidhlig - has made a special plea for the Gaelic Medium school units, whose essence to the language's survival has been emphasised to prospective legislators in the new Parliament.—See Chapter 6 for further details of the Campaign.

For the present, Gaelic Medium education has proved to be a

successful experiment, with expanding scope and favourable profile.Its assistance from public funds appears to have been justified by results, and continued sponsorship by the Scottish Office and local education authorities looks assured.

The recurrent query arising is whether dependence on those statutory bodies has limited the political influence of Scottish Gaeldom to the level of an "insider" lobby, bereft of radical thrust? Put simply, has education become another force for domination of the Scottish Gaelic world, to the point that its political teeth have been forfeited? With what voice can Scottish Gaels speak, in the event of adversity? The answers to those questions remain to be discovered, but for the present look best stocked among contingent hypotheses marked "unlikely".

NORTHERN IRELAND: One notable achievement of Ulster Gaels has been the growing Bunscoileanna movement. This initiative in Irish medium schools has grown from a single Bunscoil in 1971 to a whole new educational sector, which includes 14 Primary schools (Bunscoileanna), 2 secondary schools (Meanscoileanna) and 35 Nursery schools (Naiscoileanna). Indeed the Irish Medium schools represent Northern Ireland's fastest-growing educational sector, albeit one with whom the Department of Education experiences the most uneasy of relationships.*18

The background to this development has been traced by Maguire to the original Shaws Road (Belfast) project. *19

Earlier Gaeilgeoir initiatives in 1950s &'60s Belfast had focussed on building a self-sustaining urban Gaeltacht, whose economic and social structures would provide a durable basis for survival. The beginning of a settled Gaeilgeoir community in 1969 meant there was a demand for Irish medium education; hence the opening of the local Bunscoil Phobal Feirste and Naiscoil Bhreandain (both in Andersonstown) in 1971. Interestingly, the survival of what was initially viewed by many sympathetic observers as a brave but ultimately foolhardy exercise, served to slowly stimulate other Gaeilgeoir educational initiatives elsewhere in Belfast and throughout the Six Counties.So also did it generate confidence and a growth agenda among Gaeilgeoiri educationalists. Yet it has to be acknowledged that the success of the Andersonstown Bunscoil did not become apparent until the early 1980s. By then a whole generation of Irish Medium pupils had passed through the school, and despite a refusal of funding by the Northern Ireland Office still Bunscoil Phobal Feirste had survived and grown. Indeed state support, when eventually coming in 1984, emerged only as a corollary of the Northern Ireland Office's enthusiasm for funding the integrated - and rather middle class- Lagan College, Belfast; and in those circumstances the NIO could not credibly deny assistance to a viable Gaelic medium institution. *20

Irish Medium education was slow to develop. Over 1984/85, five new nurseries opened, three of them in Belfast; Nai -aonad Bhreandain (Andersonstown). Naiscoil Ard Eoin (Ardoyne) and Naiscoil na bhFal (Falls).The other two were Naiscoil na Rinne and Bunscoil Cholm Cille, both in Derry. Interestingly the two founding Bunscoileanna in Belfast and Derry each boast the largest pupil recruitment at present(July 1997) with 350 and 226 children respectively. *21

So also due to the 'feeder' Irish medium playschools, whose combined 1997 (July) Belfast pupil numbers in twelve schools - centred in Andersonstown, Ardoyne, Whiterock, Twinbrook, New Lodge, Lower Ormeau and Falls- reached 318. *22

Among Belfast Naiscoileanna, pupil numbers vary; with 105 children in the two Andersonstown schools, 80 in both Falls schools, 37 in the two Whiterock schools, 13 in Gort na Mona, 21 in Ardoyne, 10 in New Lodge, 10 in Lower Ormeau and 33 in Twinbrook. *23

Beyond Belfast, a further 23 Naiscoileanna are actively functioning, with five schools in Derry City covering a total of 84 pupils, and a further three in the rural county notably Maghera (two schools) and Dungiven. Other Gaelic nursery schools have emerged in Dunloy and Crumlin (both in Antrim), the four Armagh towns of Portadown, Lurgan, Camlough and Armagh city; Enniskillen,

Fermanagh; along with Downpatrick, Newry and Castlewellan, all in Down. Additionally, the Naiscoileanna movement has gained a substantial foothold in Tyrone, with nursery schools emerging in Strabane, Gortin, Dungannon,Coalisland and Castlederg.A total of 672 infants were beginning their education in Irish medium nurseries throughout the Six Counties in July 1997, with further units planned over the next three years. * 24 See Appendix 7 for full details.

It is also important to note that Irish Medium nursery schools do not receive state funding, unlike their Scottish counterparts.Hence their financial viability depends on the fundraising efforts of parents, governors and community support.

The Bunscoileanna, numbering 14 and covering 1,213 primary school children (Figures true for 1997; see Appendix 8) are also spread throughout the Six Counties. Of that number, 6 Irish medium primary schools are located in Belfast; notably in Andersonstown (350 pupils), Lower Falls (230), Lower Ormeau (36), Ardoyne (64), Twinbrook(72) and Whiterock (77), totalling some 829 pupils. *25

The remaining 384 pupils are educated at Bunscoileanna based in broadly the same areas as the gaelic nurseries, with the latter acting as 'feeder' units; notably Newry (57), Maghera (21), Coalisland (21). Dunloy (12), Strabane (7), Armagh (33), Derry (226) and Downpatrick (226). *26

It is important to acknowledge that individual school sizes correspond in two factors, age and area. Without exception, the larger schools have been those longest in existence; ie. Andersonstown (1971) and Lower Falls (1987), Belfast along with Derry(1985). Conversely, the smaller schools, like Downpatrick and Dunloy, have only been founded within the past two years from the time of writing. Location is especially relevant, since it governs the numbers of 'feeder' Gaelic nurseries, as well as prevalence of local Nationalist political culture. It is the latter which generates community support and donations, such as help each Bunscoil through its early years of self funding, before assistance - Maintained status - becomes a possibility from the Northern Ireland Department of Education.

Such recognition is dependent on minimum pupils numbers (which rarely falls below 50) and a period of self-funded viability.To date, seven of the Bunscoileanna have been granted Maintained status; notably Andersonstown, Lower Falls, Ardoyne, Twinbrook and Whiterock (all Belfast), along with Derry and Armagh. *27

Additionally,Bunscoil an Iuir, Newry, after ten years of a struggling, independent existence, and prolonged campaigns by local Gaeilgeoiri and Nationalist public representatives, has just been scheduled for Maintained status, commencing in September 1997. *28

In general, prior to the granting of state assistance, Bunscoileanna had to survive on devoted Gaeilgeoiri parents' support in each community. Although the Department of Education has recently eased pressures with its new funding policy, this has been both belated and lacking cultural even-handedness. Indeed the Department has been repeatedly accused by Gaeilgeoir educationalists of harbouring anti-Irish prejudices. This charge is based on a mixture of their non-recognition of the centra-fugal role of the Irish Medium Schools Council, plus the Department's insistence on unreasonable minimum pupil quotas . *29 The grievance is further accentuated by simultaneous N.I.O generosity to well-favoured integrated schools, so beloved of middle class suburbans.

Given developments in Gaelic nursery and primary education throughout the 1980s and ;90s, it was inevitable that, as occurred in Scotland, a secondary level Irish Medium sector would follow in the Six Counties. In 1991, Northern Ireland's first Gaelic secondary school opened on the site of the Culturlann Macadam/O'Fiaich, Belfast; enrolling some 40 pupils in three yearly streams. From the beginning, the biggest struggle was for viability. Specifically, this meant extensive fund raising, increasing pupil numbers, attracting suitable teachers, extending subject choices, and acquiring sufficient capital resources against persistent N.I.O funding refusals to enable growth. A confined premises, along with limited library and sports facilities, added to the school's early hurdles, thus taxing the best effort of parents and community fundraisers.*30

That the project succeeded is testament to the dedication and self sacrifice of parents, teachers and Belfast Gaeilgeoiri generally, as well as positive leadership shown over that critical development period by Principal, Fearghas O'hlr. Evidently their various efforts have turned a dream into something approaching a manifest reality, albeit one with much ground yet to cover.

By July 1997, Meanscoil Feirste (Belfast Irish Medium Secondary School) had recruited 230 pupils, embracing the conventional five yearly streams (ages 11 -16), and with subjects taught up to GCSE level. Additionally, it has scheduled plans for commencing sixth form studies for post-16 pupils in September 1997, offering an initial six A' Level subjects.All subjects are taught and examined through the medium of Irish, and appropriate arrangements for Irish-speaking examiners have been made with the Northern Ireland Department of Education.* 31

Most significant was the N.I.O's granting for Maintained Status for the school in 1996.*32

This valuable injection of funding, which includes salaried terms for teachers and provision of books and other resources, relieves pressure on school managers. Their next quest is to acquire an enlarged and permanent site for the Meanscoil within West Belfast, with the aim of facilitating further growth over the years ahead.*33

Given the growth in local Bunscoileanna and Naiscoileanna over the past ten years, it is realistic to assume that a whole generation of young Belfast Gaeilgeoiri will have need of the Meanscoil in times ahead.

Another developing Meanscoil feature has been its provision of Further Education courses for Belfast's Gaeilgeoir community.Additional to Irish language classes, there has been a growth in vocational and A' Level courses; something that has been given fresh impetus by recent advances in secondary level Irish Medium education. Gearoid O' Caireallain anticipates that further growth patterns over the next decade will necessitate the creation of some kind of third level Irish medium institution, perhaps in association with Belfast Further Education Institute or one of the North's two universities.*34

This proposition, if a little ambitious on the basis of current numbers, nevertheless looks felicitous in the longer term.

There is a second, smaller Meanscoil in Derry.However, with just 56 pupils on its rolls (July 1997),Meanscoil Dhoire has much basic development yet to realise before state funding becomes a realistic possibility.*35

Yet even its prospects are not without hope, in view of the substantial numbers of Derry children being educated at local Naiscoileanna and Bunscoil Cholm Cille, as well as similar initiatives in adjoining Maghera.Additional plans are scheduled for opening a small Meanscoil at Newry in 1998, to take pupils emerging from the local Bunscoil an Iuir. While this project has yet to become functional, the growing uptake of Irish Medium education at primary and nursery levels in Newry, Armagh, Camlough and Castlewellan (all within travelling distance), make advance secondary level planning for a South Down Meanscoil wholly appropriate.*36

Additional overview factors are relevant to this examination of Gaelic Medium education in the North.

First, Northern Ireland's Irish Medium schools are represented by their own, Belfast-based umbrella organisation, An Comhairle don Oideachas Lan- Ghaelige -Gaeloiliuinit (Council for Irish Medium Education). This body, which was founded in 1991, has the double task of representing Gaeilgeoir school interests to the N.I Education Department (a role the latter has failed to recognise), while also projecting and co-ordinating the various Naiscoileanna and Bunscoileanna across the Six Counties. Additionally, it must give assistance to the two Meanscoileanna, and encourage such new initiatives as periodically emerge, within limited resources.

For its work, Gaeloiliuint has an office in Andersonstown, along with a full time small staff. The key post of Development Officer is presently held by energetic Derry Gaeilgeoir, Cathail O'Donnaighle, whose principal concern lies with assisting new Nais/Bun/Mean scoil projects. An additional post of Education Officer is funded by the N.I Department for Education, and held by former Belfast Institute Irish Studies lecturer, Peadar MacMuiris. More recently, the N.I Department of the Environment began funding a Children's Events Organiser post, held by Antoine O'Muireagahin; and in 1997 funding for a temporary administrative post came from the Belfast European Partnership.*37

As regards Gaeloiliuint's own income, this has been precarious. Additional to donations and self-generated revenue, Gaeloiliuint has benefited from two grants; one from the 'Doors of Hope' social Trust, and another from the American-Ireland Fund, created in the aftermath of the Anglo-Irish Agreement to assist worthy community projects in Northern Ireland.* 38

Second, the Irish Medium schools are all non-denominational, with an open policy on recruitment. However, in keeping with political realities, almost all pupils are drawn from Nationalist (mainly Catholic) families, as it is from that community that demand for Gaelic education exists.Moreover, though not subject to any clerical direction,Bunscoileanna and Meanscoileanna pupils are provided with what is effectively Catholic religious instruction, along with Sacramental induction (ie. First Communion,Confession and Confirmation) and more moral guidance. However, R.C catachetical teaching is not a deliberate policy; instead it reflects Irish Medium uptake. In any case, religious instruction attendance is voluntary, and Gaeloiliuint organisers have indicated that alternative, specifically Protestant, religious instruction will be made available, subject to future demand.

Third, Irish Medium schools fall outside the mainstream Church sector; with Catholic Maintained schools constituting their main rivals. The latter are well established as mainstream educators of the Nationalist community, possessing a distinctive Catholic-Irish ethos, plus a solid track record of teaching the Irish language, arts,history and Gaelic sports.*39

Also, the R.C. hierarchy's preference for Church schools is no small matter among Catholic parents in the Six Counties, where various surveys show average Mass attendance at over 85% of the Catholic population. * 40

Accordingly, only the most committed Gaeilgeoiri will brave the privations, costs and uncertainties of new units, which do not command whole-hearted endorsement from their bishops.For such people, subsistence comforts are a worthy premium for the benefits of a linguistic and cultural identity bequeathed to future generations of Ulster Gaeilgeoiri.

Fourth, servicing the Irish Medium schools by government bodies and the educational establishment has been belated and rather basic.A 1995 Gaeloiliuint paper noted an N.I.O announcement of £150,000 expenditure that year on Irish medium education.*41

While welcoming the initial revenue, Gaeloiliuint decried the 0.5 million needing to be self generated, comparing their position to that of the Integrated Educational Council, for whom NIO funding enabled the employment of twelve officers.Although subsequent public funding has reduced the gulf, nevertheless the perception of political hostility towards the Irish language among British ministers and their Stormont advisers firmly characterises Gaeloiliuint statements.*42

Of particular concern is the NIO's failure to publish the 1993 document, 'Athbhreithniu Polasai i leith na Gaeilige/A review of Policy in regard to the Irish language', commissioned on Gaeloiliuint's persistent urgings.Nor is there any specific NIO budget for the Irish language, as happens for Gaidhlig and Welsh.*43

At the same time, certain miscellaneous factors provide positive omens. For one thing, St Mary's College, Belfast, now offers a B.Ed degree for Irish language teachers through Gaelic medium. This comes in addition to the College's existing Celtic Studies courses, which have functioned for over thirty years. Also, St Mary's are now placing Irish medium B.Ed. and P.G.C.E.(postgraduate) students at various Bun/Meanscoileanna on teaching practice.Such connections strengthen manpower links, while elevating the professional status of the Irish medium sector.More generally, the growing appeal of Irish language studies in schools and colleges throughout Northern Ireland has produced a 46% increase in GCSE entries, from 1,518 in 1988 to the record 2,215 candidates emerging in 1996.*44

Such developments have enhanced the Irish language image over recent years, against the prejudices of NIO policymakers and hostility of Unionist critics.

CONCLUSIONS: From evidence presented in this chapter, the following conclusions may be drawn.

First, Gaelic Medium education enhances the state of the native language in both countries. It generates demand for books and other resources, while also obliging the educational authorities to increase the numbers of trained teachers. Additionally, it has created specialist educational sectors in both countries, which are achieving steady growth. Moreover,, it is to be reasonably expected that growth levels will be sustained over the ensuing decades, given current trends in recruitment.

Second, Gaelic Medium education requires Government aid and also community support if it is to have a future. This has been largely forthcoming in Western Scotland, where the Scottish Office and various Highlands & Islands local authorities have collaborated in pursuit of the overriding goal. However, similar support has come only from the Nationalist population in Northern Ireland, where Gaelic culture and the language are among defining characteristics of political nationalism. Notwithstanding the obstacles, Gael Uladh has succeeded in guiding its Irish medium schools sector through an uncertain birth to an increasingly confident and structured life, with an assured future.

Third, by generating whole new sectors in both countries, Gaelic Medium education represents a long term 'fait accompli'. Its growth cannot be easily stopped - as shown by the Ulster Gaeilgeoiri experience - by either a lukewarm public sector, hostile political lobby, or scarcity of public funding.Moreover, it is in the Gaelic Medium programme that Scottish and Irish Gaeldom have developed their most potent strategies for enabling the language to survive the vast commercial, literary, media and political pressures towards anglicisation.

While the ramifications of a budding Bun/Meanscioleanna sector looks healthy for the future of Irish Nationalism, conversely the relatively apolitical Scottish Gaels cannot be discounted. The latter's partisan neutrality might well experience reappraisal in light of reviving sinews of political nationalism presently affecting Scotland as she prepares to enter the third millennium. While the schools must refrain from party polemics, nevertheless the presence of a growing retinue of Gaelic speakers must surely bode some consequences for perceptions of Scottish nationhood.It remains to be seen where this may lead in the future?

FOOTNOTES AND REFERENCES

1.Hindley (1990); Chaps 4&5.

2.(i) Hindley (1990); Chaps 3 & 5. (ii) MacKinnon (1991); Chaps 6-8.

3.Western Isles Bilingual Education Project; Stirling University survey published 1987:- see MacKinnon (1991), pp. 142-146.

4.Dr Anne Lorne Gillies contested The Western Isles as SNP candidate in the 1997 British General Election; coming second to outgoing/re-elected MP, Dr Calum Macdonald (Labour).She enjoys respect for her Doctoral and post-Doctoral research in the area of Gaelic medium education.

5.See MacKinnon (1991); pp. 173-175.

6. Maguire (1991);Chaps 4&5.

7.Maguire 91991); Chap 12.

8. (i)MacKinnon (1991); pp. 142-153. (ii)Discussions with Donald John Maciver, Dolina Macleod, Alan Campbell.and Peadar Morgan.

9. See McKee, Contemporary Politics (1995);pp.100-101

10.Figures supplied by Donald John Maciver; Correspondence 2nd July, 1997.

11. Ibid.

12. Discussions with Donald John Maciver,28th July 1997.

13.Correspondence, D.J.Maciver/V.McKee, 2nd July,1997.

14.Comhairle Nan Eilean Leiamheas Buileachadh Poileasaidh Foghlam Da-Chananach,Sultain, 1992,pp.9-10 (Ang Bilingual Education Implementation Review, Sept.1992)

15.Correspondence,D.JMaciber/V McKee, 2nd July, 1997

16.Figures supplied by Mr Keith Scammell, An Runai/Secretary, Comhairle Nan Sgoiltean Araich/Gaelic Pre-School Council; correspondence - 8th July, 1997.

17.Discussions with Mr Keith Scammell; 7th July, 1997.

18.Figures supplied by Gaeloiliuint officers, Peadar MacMuiris and Cathail O'Donnaighle; memorandum 30th June, 1997.

19. Maguire (1991); Chaps 3&4.

20.McKee, Contemporary Politics (1995); p.103.

21.Gaeloiliuint memorandum. 30th June, 1997.

22.Ibid

23.Ibid

24.Ibid

25.Ibid

26.Ibid

27.Ibid

28.(i) Ibid

(ii)Discussions with Cathail O'Donnaighle and Peadar MacMuiris, 1st July, 1997. (iii)Discussions with Gearoid O'Caireallain, 7th January, 1994 and 21st July,1997 (iv)Discussions with Patsy McGlone, 19th September, 1994 and 2nd July, 1997.

29. (i)Gaeloiliuint memorandum. (ii)N.I Dept. of Education policy was also criticised by a range of interviewees, including Patsy McGlone, Cathail O'Donnaighle, Gearoid O'Caireallain, Peadar MacMuiris and Hugh Carr (Discussion, 8th May, 1994)

30. Discussions (i) Gearoid O'Cearaillean, 7th January, 1994, and 21st July, 1997. (ii) Cathail O'Donnaighle and Peadar MacMuiris, 1st July, 1997.

31.Ibid.

32. See Gaeloiliuint memorandum.

33.Discussions, Gearoid O'Caireallain and Cathail O'Donnaighle.

34.Discussion Gearoid O'Caireallain/V McKee, 21st July, 1997.

35.Ref. Gaeloiliuint memorandum,supplemented by up-dated information received in discussions with Gearoid O'Caireallain, Cathail O'Donnaighle and Peadar McMuiris.

36.Ibid

37.Discussion with Cathail O'Donnaighle, 1st July, 1997.

38.Ibid .

39.Ref. Ophsal Commission Report.

40.Ref.Diocesan records, Down & Connor ; pub.Catholic Media Office Ireland.

41.Gaeloiliuint memorandum.

42. Ibid

43.Ibid.

44.Northern Ireland GCSE Irish Language Chief Examiner's Report, 1996.

CHAPTER 6
COMPARATIVE ASSESSMENTS & CONCLUSIONS

There is a general predisposition among nationalists everywhere to view their own affairs in isolation from those of the wider political community. This tendency suggests that every situation is without precedent; hence few if any lessons need be drawn from experiences elsewhere. In reality, and notwithstanding the specific traits of each conflict, such parochial thinking is confounded by the weight of opposing evidence.Hence even a seemingly unique phenomenon as that of Celtic cultural politics within the British state has comparative dimensions. Moreover, the issue of minority languages and cultures has been addressed at European level, both by guardians of the Convention on Human Rights and the European Union. Although progress may be at an early stage, nevertheless the issues raised by resurgent Gaelicism have been addressed in forums beyond the sovereignty of the British and Irish states

European Dimension The Gaels of Ireland - North and South - hold common ground with some thirty four recognised communities in Western Europe. Other Celtic language communities include 503,549 Census-recorded native Welsh speakers in Wales, along with 500,000 native speaking Bretons of Brittany. Spain hosts some 600,000 Basques, 7,000,000 Catalans and 1,500,000 Galacians, thereby raising culture and language to the level of major constitutional issues, for which autonomy arrangements have been designed. France has a 90,000 strong Basque community, plus 150,000 native-speaking Corsicans; while elsewhere there are 110,000 Serbians in eastern Germany, 300,000

Frisians in the Netherlands and 40,000 Rhaetians in Switzerland. *1

European initiatives have been recently forthcoming, albeit lacking enforcement authority. The first was the European Parliament's adoption in 1981 of the Arfe Resolution, with amendments in 1983, which implored national governments to legislate rights and provisions for minority languages in education, broadcasting, social and political affairs. A similar resolution was adopted by the Council of Europe in 1981, followed by a working party on Regional or Minority Languages, who drafted a code of practice. Eventually, in 1992, there followed the Council's adoption of the European Charter for Regional or Minority Languages, binding member states to a basic standard of provision for minority language communities in educational, cultural and administrative affairs. *2

Significantly, as has already been mentioned, the United Kingdom abstained in the final vote, as, surprisingly, did the Irish representative. Earlier, in 1982, the European Bureau for Lesser Spoken Languages had been founded with a permanent headquarters in Dublin, and grant assistance from the European Union. This body supports various minority language and cultural initiatives through its public platform, as well as organising conferences and seminars, like those events held in Stornoway, Isle of Lewis, earlier listed. It further assists with providing research and publishing outlets for minority language/cultural communities and their lobbyists, additional to lobbying national governments on their behalf.

Accordingly, the challenges facing Scottish and Irish Gaelic linguists and cultural activists merits a wider European perspective, on account of similar factors prevailing throughout Western Europe. European influence has generally been positive, through having pressurised various governments into making accommodations with their indigenous minorities. Therefore, Gaeldom's experience has been typical, albeit at variable paces between Scotland and Northern Ireland.

European support has boosted the language/cultural minorities cause, and its permanent body has had the effect of overseeing their interests while also providing a useful focal point. Also, the permanent Bureau has achieved some co-ordination between various communities. Yet on an overall basis, those innovations represent only minimal progress. It is unclear as to how far the European Union/Court can continue to wreak concessions, and what effect these may have on cultural development. For one thing, minority language groups do not currently constitute a priority in either E.U or Council affairs. However, with the European Union expanding ever-further eastwards, and the admission of Turkey with its Kurdish minority and former Warsaw Pact countries containing substantial national minorities, a distinct possibility in the medium term future, it is likely that the minorities question will rise in significance. For the present, European minority language/cultural communities are at the mercy of their national governments, whose willingness to make accommodations varies from state to state. For example, the hostile policy of Franco's regime towards Spanish Basques and Catalans in the aftermath of Spain's democratisation, following the Dictator's death in 1975. France has made limited and rather belated concessions to its Corsican minority, largely in a bid to stave of the tide of Corsican separatism.*3

Even the native-speaking communities of North and mid-Wales wrestled their various concessions from a reluctant British government through the 1970s and '80s, on the back of Plaid Cymru's post 1967 electoral advances and a sustained campaign by the Welsh Language Society. *4

The gains included statutory equality for Welsh in the public domain,enhanced funding and entitlements to Welsh education, and a shared TV channel for Welsh speakers.

Accordingly, the experiences of Scottish and Northern Irish Gaels were not without precedent elsewhere in Western Europe.Nor are there contrasting traits - notably nationalistic (Irish) and apolitical/moderate (Scottish) - wholly unique either. Yet the small numbers of both communities, along with their determined pace of development does rank as exceptional. The notion of a historically repressed heritage in both countries elevates the Gaelic cause to a high moral position within the wider European body of regional/minority language communities and suppressed nations, putting them on a par with others demanding justice for their language(s) and culture(s). Moreover, the association between cultural Gaelicism and political nationalism in Ireland, along with Northern Ireland's high profile over recent decades, adds to Gaeldom's international appeal. It remains to be seen where this course shall lead over future years, especially as the European Union develops quasi-federal political structures, with the potential for nationalist unrest that such a prospect holds.

The international impact of bilingualism is considerable too, especially at local council level. One major effect of the two bilingual councils, Western Isles and Newry & Mourne, is to have focussed attention on the 'regionalised' Celtic cultures within the British state, with their many counterparts elsewhere in Europe. Both councils counter-poise their respective anglophile establishments, and along with catering for local community demands, they also provide symbolic monuments to the continuing vitality of the Gaelic language and culture in the Hebrides and Northern Ireland. West Belfast's Gaeltacht community, complete with its schools and evolving socio-economic infrastructures, has also contributed to the same revivalist phenomenon. So also does the Gaelic medium education movement, along with Gaelic sports, music, theatre and media augment the process in both countries. All those factors, enable a degree of recognition from the wider European community, several of whose countries compose minority cultures which must be accommodated in equitable fashion. Accordingly, given the gradual process of political convergence within Europe, the spotlight looks likely to continue its focus on minority language communities across the region. So too are the European Parliament and Council likely to remain forums for the assertion of their claims, with the considerable moral authority that both institutions enjoy.However, it remains a moot point as to whether in the British case European pressures underlay any of the funding, educational or enabling reforms to concede to Gaeldom in either country. The Scottish reforms appear to have been won by the merits and persistence of lobbying by An Comunn Gaidhealach and its sister groups, plus a willingness to co-operate in educational and cultural programmes jointly managed with various statutory authorities. In the Northern Irish case, concessions to the Irish language and Gaelic cultural lobby appear to have been wrenched by a combination of Northern Nationalist politicians, sympathisers at Westminster,Dublin's persistent voice and sustained community efforts by Ulster Gaeilgeoiri. *5

If there were any potent international pressures, the more influential would appear to have been those from America, especially in the aftermath of the Anglo-Irish Agreement.*6

Put simply, Europe provides a moral framework for action, but little else.

Future Prospects and Challenges: For the future, European institutions would seem well placed to act as guarantors of the minority language and cultural communities, but Scottish and Northern Irish Gaels need only look to Europe for symbolic support. Their major gains have been self-attained, with patrons and campaigns that proved effective. While government no longer raises fundamental obstacles, it remains to be seen whether civic culture in Scotland and Northern Ireland will prove amenable to Gaelicism? The signs look more promising in Scotland than Northern Ireland. As has been shown throughout this account,Scottish education, publishers, the media, churches, theatrical and political worlds have all moved to an accommodation with the resurgent Gaelic language and culture. However in Northern Ireland the picture is different. Ulster Unionist political strength, though no longer constituting the dominant monopoly of Stormont days, nevertheless is still a formidable force, and remains pitted against Gaelic culture in the Six

Counties.Moreover, while there appear to be definite signs of a broadcasting market for the Gaelic language, such changes are relatively minor and confined to Unionist 'Progressives' and a few liberal minds at the Northern Ireland Office at present. However such hopes were dashed by the peculiar decision by the Northern Ireland Fair Employment Agency in August 1997, to brand Irish notices at Queens University as sectarian. The latter action shows a mixture of ignorance and naivety.* 7

Indeed this display of cultural ineptitude by the Agency also has the effect of redefining political boundaries for the Irish language within the Six Counties' civic culture.Hence even Northern Ireland's liberal watchdogs cannot be relied upon to recognise the legitimate entitlements of Ulster Gaeilgeoiri to appropriate recognition for the native language and culture. Such a state of affairs does nothing to reduce the alienation of Nationalists generally and Gaeilgeoiri particularly.

Despite a shared historical experience of suppression, the diversity of political opinion within the Gaelic movements of Scotland and Ireland shows their contemporary political agendas to be different. Nor do they make similar assumptions about the good faith of the British government. Among Scottish Gaels, the sectional lobbying of An Comunn Gaidhealach, along with its distance from nationalist politics, has rendered a rich yield of grants, educational recognition and administrative favour. Such has also meant that relations between the Scottish Office and Scottish Gaeldom, with all the symbolic gestures of favour that have resulted from the latter. Perhaps the most evident of these is royal patronage; hence the naming of Scottish Gaeldom's premier cultural event 'The Royal National Mod'. Similar patronage for Gaelic sports, musical or language events in Northern Ireland would be inconceivable in even the most liberal climate. Conversely, the Ulster Gaeilgeoir movement is anti-establishment and has to face a hostile Unionist establishment, itself no friend of Gaelic causes. The West Belfast Gaeilgeoir initiative, along with the Irish Medium Schools movement, La, Glor na Gael and Sinn Fein activists represent the radical wing of Gael Uladh. At the same time, Newry & Mourne Council, with its SDLP dominance and Comhaltas Uladh influences, along with the Irish language sector at St Mary's College/Q.U.B, Belfast, and the University of Ulster, present a more pragmatic, civic-orientated character. So also does the more substantial voice emanating from the Gaelic Athletic Association in the Six Counties.*8

Overall, therefore, Scottish Gaels have opted for co-operation and cultural projection very much in the mould of Wyn Grant's thesis of an 'insider' sectional lobby.*9

By contrast, Ulster Gaels are a product of the Nationalist political culture - inclusive of its moderate and militant strands - that has been challenging the British and Unionist establishment ever since the partition of Ireland in 1921. Their gains have been less,but by articulating their case culturally and politically, financial aid has been attained, as has grudging recognition from the Northern Ireland Office. Significantly, both Gaelic communities now enjoy the enhanced legitimacy accorded to minor languages/cultures by the European Union and Council of Europe.

In his essay on the politics of French Quebec, James Tully argues that linguistic/cultural minorities often articulate their political agendas through cultural channels.* 10

Therefore nationalist movements like the Quebecan separatists may appeal effectively to a cultural strain at variance with the dominant culture. Moreover, by linking culture to constitution and political system, separatists may encourage feelings of alienation within their community. While Quebec does not wholly parallel with Scotland and only broadly with Northern Ireland, nonetheless Tully's observations are relevant to an understanding of language and identity in minority cultures. Historically, Gaeldom has bequeathed legacies to Scotland and Northern Ireland. Initially there was Crown repression in both countries, followed by diminishing numbers of native speakers throughout the nineteenth and twentieth centuries. Thereafter the similarities end.The identification of Gaelic revivalism with separatism was inevitable in Ireland, but, as shown earlier, did not mark Scottish nationalism in the same way. Indeed Scotland's nineteenth century anglophile-Unionist political establishment, with its scarce tolerance for the Gaelic Highlands and Hebrides, - so aptly described by Glasgow University's eminent historian, the late Professor George Pryde - had defined political structures in terms that would have consigned any exclusive alliance, contemporary or future, between Gaeldom and Scottish nationalism to the margins of national life. *11

E. Gellner's study of comparative nationalism contemplated the psychological link between political and cultural nationalism, which he argued, augmented the former's appeal. *12

This was especially relevant to popular culture elements like language, which had been repressed.Gellner's thesis is borne out by the Northern Irish experience. Equally, Irish Unionists' reticence is due to a suspicion of the culture from which nationalism draws much life blood. Conversely, in Scotland, despite the historic Gaelic hegemony of early medieval times, in fact so distant is that link with contemporary Scottish culture that Gaeldom's principal appeal is restricted to the West Highlands and Hebrides, plus the ex-patriate community in Glasgow. This factor has militated against an alliance between Scottish Gaeldom and Scottish nationalism on the Irish model. However, the same factor has enabled Scottish Gaels to lobby for recognition and state funding, free from the political limitations applying in Northern Ireland. Indeed the achievements of An Comunn Gaidhealach and - recently -Comhairle Nan Eilean in education, arts and broadcasting says much about their promotional worth.Moreover, by fashioning a positive Gaelic consensus among all major Scottish political parties, An Comunn Gaidhealach and Comunn na Gaidhlig have ensured that Gaelic funding does not become a hostage to the fortunes of changing political occupancy at the Scottish Office, nor moods of a future Scottish Parliament. By contrast, lesser benefits have accrued to Ulster Gaels, whose links with political nationalism have both popularised and penalised their appeal. *13

The most recent experience at Queens University would appear to highlight that dilemma.

Since spring 1997, a campaign for secure status has been pursued by Comunn na Gaidhlig, directed at all the Scottish parties and other policymakers concerned with the creation and role of the Parliament.*14

The latter has included a bid for legal recognition of Gaelic by the Parliament, something CNG would prefer to see exemplified by the adoption of a Gaelic translation of all its proceedings.*15

More particularly, CNG's campaign is specifically concerned with protecting the budgets, entitlements, growth targets and overall status of the language under the planned new constitutional arrangements for the future government of Scotland.*16

As for Ulster Gaeldom, its major challenge over times ahead lies with developing the Irish Medium schools sector, which will require more funds and enabling entitlements form the Northern Ireland Office. The various consultative mechanisms developed by the Anglo-Irish Agreement enable the Irish government to extend their lobbyist influence to matters of culture and language, such as affects the Nationalist community. Accordingly, under those conditions, it is unlikely that Ulster Gaeldom will ever slip back to the state of decline that was its lot during the hostile years of Unionist government from Stormont. Moreover, given the modest advances made by Nationalists over the past three decades, along with their increasing demographic strength, even the civic culture of Unionism has had to make accommodations with Gaelic culture and the Irish language.*17

Such a change is underlined by the slow entry of Gaelic sports and Irish music to the Northern media (see chapters 3 & 4), along with the rising numbers of Catholics appearing in senior positions across the entire public sector spectrum in Northern Ireland, including the BBC-N.I., Ulster Television and the Northern Ireland Civil Service.

This legacy of the early civil rights campaigns and subsequent Westminster reforms, along with the Anglo-Irish Agreement, is now being experienced in terms more positive than ever before to Irish culture, sports and the language.*18

The support of all-Ireland bodies like Conradh na Gaeilge and Gael Linn, along with other sister groups like Comhaltas Ceolteori na hEireann and Cumann Luthchleas Gael, as well as the Irish government has provided Gael Uladh with a degree of fraternity that lessened its isolation, even at the nadir of its fortunes during the Stormont years. Now with the recent advent of Teilifis na Gaeilge in the Twenty Six Counties, and a successful weekly Irish language newspaper published from Belfast, the renewed confidence of Gaelgeoiri in both parts of Ireland has been well founded. Put simply, with the lot of Northern Nationalists having improved immeasurably, Ulster Gaelgeoiri seem to have emerged from their 'dark age' into more promising times.

More generally, the Gaelic language cannot indefinitely feed off Nationalist appeal in Northern Ireland, nor the Highlands-Hebridean social infra-structure in Scotland. Yet despite the pessimism of Reg Hindley about the future of Irish Gaelic, a view linked to declining numbers of native speakers, in fact developing Gaelic education and cultural activities augur well for long term survival.*18

Perhaps those like Hindley, engaged in writing Gaeldom's obituary in both countries, might usefully take account of the evolving socio-economic infra-structures being laid by Gaelgeoiri from various sectors. Their conclusions might thus be less adamant about Gaeldom's inevitable demise.

In that final analysis, Gaelic education and cultural pursuits need an appeal in both Northern Ireland and Scotland that is broadened beyond conventional bounds. Plainly, the traditional political parameters have outlived their usefulness. This book has attempted to show how the foundations for Gaeldom's survival into the third millennium have been painstakingly laid. It now remains to be seen how far they are utilised by both nations.

FOOTNOTES AND REFERENCES

1.See *(i)European Community (Union) Commission,Summary Report on Minority Cultural/Language Groups, 1986. (ii)Statesman's Yearbook, 1988-89, in Hindley, pp.233-34.*

2.See *European Commission for Minority Languages Report, 1992.* 3.*(i)V.Bogdanor 'Federalism and Devolution:Some Judicial and Political Problems', in R.Morgan (ed.) Regionalism in European Politics (London, 1986) (ii)R Wardhaugh Languages in Competition,(Oxford 1987) (iii) S Rokkan and D.W. Urwin (eds) The Politics of Territorial Identity: Studies in European Regionalism (London, 1982)*

4.*See (i) D.Balsom 'Plaid Cymru: the Welsh National Party' in Multi-Party Britain; in H.M.Drucker (ed) Multi-Party Britain (1979) (ii) P.Trudgill (ed) Language in the British Isles; (Cambridge, 1984).*

5.*See (i)Maguire (1991); Chaps 3-5. (ii) McKee; Contemporary Politics (1995).*

6. *Ibid.*

7.*(i)Reports, Irish News (Belfast) ; 20th&21st August, 1997. (ii)Patsy McGlone 'Two Identities must be Recognised' ; Irish News, 8th September, 1997.*

8.*See (i)V.McKee Contemporary Politics (1995), pp.108-110.*

(ii)The Northern GAA has availed itself of various grants and entitlements emerging from public bodies in the Six Counties, eg,Ulster Sports Council, local council awards, Northern Ireland Department of Education etc; accepting the restraints that go with those awards for sport and culture.

9.*Grant (1995) ;Chaps 3 &4.*

10.*James Tully 'The Crisis of Identification: the case of Canada"; Political Studies, Vol, 42 Special Issue, 1994.*

11.*George Pryde (1962); Chaps xii & xiii.*

12.*E Gellner Nations and Nationalism (Oxford, 1993).*

13.*V McKee (i)Contemporary Politics (1995),pp 110-111. (ii) 'Historic Overview of Gaeldom decline in Scotland and Ireland';Questions of Ideology, Occasional Papers in Government series, Vol.3 pub. South Bank University, London, May 1994.*

14.*(i)Annual Report of Comunn na Gaidhlig, inclusive of Secure Status section, 1997. (ii)Athaisg na Comhdhail: Congress Report on Community Aspiration Towards Secure Status for Gaelic; Comunn na Gaidhlig, 20th June, 1997, Inverness. (iii) 'Framework for Growth: A National Policy for Gaelic Education' Discussion Paper, Comunn na Gaidhlig, 1997.*

15. *(i) Ibid. (ii) Discussions with Alan Campbell, Chief Executive, CNG.*

16.*Ibid.*

17. *For a detailed analysis of the slow retreat of Unionism from its previous hegemony, see; (i) B.O'Leary & J.McGarry (eds.), 1993. (ii) G.Mc Guire (1991) ; Chaps 2-4, concerning the Irish language specifically.*

18. *(i) Ibid. (ii) Opshal Commission Report.*

19. *Hindley (1990); concluding chapter.*

GLOSSARY

SCOTLAND/ALBANNAICH

An Comunn Gaidhealach -

Founded in 1891; Scotland's oldest Gaelic national lobby group. Head office at Inverness.

Gaelic Society of London -

ACG's London sister group, catering for Gaelic migrants in the UK capital, but also exerting a subtle influence in lobbying Government.

Comunn na Gaidhlig -

Council of the Gaels. An umbrella body, formed the mid-1980s, with Scottish Office grant aid, aiming to be a co-ordinator of the various Gaelic groups. In recent times CNG has also acted as the voice of Gaeldom. Head office at Inverness.

Comunn na Canain Albannaich -

A 1980s radical Scottish Gaelic campaigning body, modelled on the Welsh Language Society.

Comhairle Nan Sgoiltean Araich -

Gaelic Medium Playgroups Council, based at Inverness.

Comunn an Luchd-Ionnsachaidh -

Gaelic Learners Association, based at Dingwall.

Comhairle Nan Eilean -

Western Isles Council, Stornoway, Isle of Lewis; officially bilingual, founded 1975.

Gaidhealtachd -

A residential community of Gaelic speakers.

IRELAND/EIREANN

Bord na Gaeilge -

Government advisory body for Irish language affairs in Southern Ireland.

Conradh na Gaeilge -

Gaelic League; founded in 1891, and Ireland's oldest and premier lobby for the Irish language. Based in Dublin, but presently with a Belfast president.

Comhaltas Uladh -

Recognised since 1926 as the Ulster affiliate of the Gaelic League.

Comhairle an Iuir agus Mhorn -

Newry and Mourne Council, Co. Down. The first official bilingual local authority in Northern Ireland.

Cumann Luthchleas Gael -

Gaelic Athletic Association (GAA). The promotional and governing body for Gaelic football and hurling; Ireland's two national sports. Founded in 1884, it is Ireland's largest sporting body with active organisations in each of the 32 counties.

Glor na nGael -

An independent Six Counties Irish language body, mainly concerned with providing Irish teaching to the wider community. Very active in Belfast.

Gael Linn -

An Irish language action group, working in both North and South.

Gaeltacht -

A community of Irish speakers.

Gaeilgeoir -

Term used to describe an Irish speaker or advocate.

La -

Irish language weekly newspaper, published in Belfast.

Uladh -

Ulster

BIBLIOGRAPHY

NEWSPAPERS AND PERIODICALS

Aberdeen Press and Journal, The Scotsman, Oban Times, West Highland Free Press, The Herald, Stornoway Gazette, Inverness Courier, Highland News, Radical Scotland.
Irish News, Newsletter, Belfast Telegraph, Andersonstown News, La, Irish Times, Irish World, Irish Press, Fortnight.

Irish Political Studies, Journal of West European Politics, Contemporary Politics, Political Studies UK, Politics Review, Social Studies Review, Contemporary Record, The Modern Scot, Municipal Journal, Irish Review, History Today, Scottish Gaelic Studies, Ulster Folklife, Studies in Scottish Literature, Scottish Historical Review.

PUBLICATIONS

A. Alcock, B. Taylor and J. Weldon - The Future of Cultural Minorities (Macmillan 1979; London)
An Comunn Gaidealach - An Comunn Gaidhealach: The First Hundred Years 1891-1991 (ACG 1991; Inverness.)
John Bannerman - Studies in the History of Dalriada (Scottish Academic Press 1974; Edinburgh).
J.C. Beckett - The Making of Modern Ireland (Faber, 1996; London.)
Jack Brand - The National Movement in Scotland (Routledge and Kegan, Paul, 1978; London.)
Commission of the European Communities - Linguistic Minorities in Countries Belonging to the European Community (Instituto Della Enciclopedia Italiana, 1986; Rome.)
Peter Beresford Ellis - The Celtic Revolution: A study in anti-imperialism (Ceridigon, 1985; Wales)
Paul Bew and Henry Patterson - The British State and the Ulster Crisis: From Wilson to Thatcher (London, 1985.)
H.M. Drucker - Multi-Party Britain (Macmillan, 1979; London)
Owen Dudley Edwards - A Claim of Right for Scotland (Polygon, London; 1988)

European Charter for Regional or Minority Languages, 1992.
Michael Farrell - Northern Ireland: The Orange State (Pluto, London; 1976.)
R.F. Foster - Modern Ireland, 1600-1972 (Allen Lane, London; 1988).
E. Gellner - Nations and Nationalism (Oxford University Press; 1983.)
Wyn Grant - Pressure Groups, Politics and Democracy in Britain (Harverster/Wheatsheaf; London; 1995.)
Reg Hindley - Death of the Irish Language: A Qualified Obituary (Routledge, London; 1990.)
James Hunter - The Making of the Crofting Community (John Donald, Edinburgh; 1976.)
James Kellas - The Scottish Political System (Cambridge University Press, Cambridge; 1989.)
Kenneth MacKinnon - Gaelic: A Past and Future Prospect (Saltire, Edinburgh; 1991.)
J.D. Mackie - A History of Scotland (Penguin, London; 1991.)
Vincent McKee - Politics of the Gaelic Language in Northern Ireland and the Scottish Hebrides: Historical Overview (Southbank University, London 1994.)
Gabrielle Maguire - Our Own Language: An Irish Initiative (Clevedon, Belfast; 1991.)
Michael Montgomery - The Anglicisation of Scots in Seventeenth Century Ulster; (Studies in Scottish Literature, 1991.)
Sighle Nic An Ultaigh - O Shiol go Blath: The Down GAA History (Down GAA, 1990.)
K. Nicholls - Gaelic and Gaelicised Ireland in the Middle Ages (Gill and Macmillan, Dublin; 1972.)
Seamas O'Casaide - The Irish Language in Belfast and County Down (Dublin, 1930.)
Eamonn O'Ciossan - Buried Alive: A Reply to Reg Hindley (Dail Ui Chadian pamphlet, 1991; Dublin.)
Brian O'Cuiv - A View of the Irish Language (Irish Government Stationary Office, 1969; Dublin.)
Tomas O'Fiaich - The Language and Political History (in A View of the Irish Language, Brian O'Cuiv, 1969, Stationary Office, Dublin.)
Brendan O'Leary and John McGarry - The Future of Northern Ireland (Oxford, Clarendon, 1990.)

P. O'Snodaigh - Hidden Ulster (Clodhanna Teo, 1973; Belfast.)
Torkel Opsahl - The Opsahl Report on Northern Ireland, edited by Andy Pollak (Lilliput/Initiative, 1992 and 1993; Dublin.)
Richard Parry - Scottish Political Facts (Clark, 1988; Edinburgh.)
George Pryde - Scotland From 1603 to the Present Day: A New History (Nelson, 1962; Edinburgh.)
P.S. Robinson - The Scots Language in Seventeenth Century Ulster (Ulster Folklife Vol 35, 1989.)
S. Rokkan and D.W. Urwin - The Politics of Territorial Identity: Studies in European Regionalism (Sage, 1982, London.)
ATQ Stewart - The Narrow Ground: Aspects of Ulster, 1609-1969 (Faber, 1977; London.)
Donald Stewart - A Scot at Westminster (Catlone, Nova Scotia; 1994.)
P. Trudgill - Language in the British Isles (CUP, Cambridge; 1984.)
James Tully - The Crisis of Identification: The case of Canada (Political Studies Vol 42, Special Issue, 1994.)
R. Wardaugh - Languages in Competition (Oxford, Blackwell; 1987.)
CMJ Withers - Gaelic in Scotland 1698-1981: The Geographical History of a Language (John Donald, 1984; Edinburgh.)
J.N. Wolfe - Government and Nationalism in Scotland (Edinburgh University Press, 1969; Edinburgh.)

APPENDIX 1

DR. CROKE'S LETTER

At the founding of Cumann Luthchleas Gael/Gaelic Athletic Association (GAA) in Thurles, Co Tipperary, Ireland, the following letter was received from the Most Rev Dr TW Croke, RC Archbishop of Cashel and Emily.

To: Mr Michael Cusack
Hon. Secretary, GAA.
18th September, 1884.

My Dear Sir,

I beg to acknowledge the receipt of your communication inviting me to become a patron of the Gaelic Athletic Association, of which you are it appears, the Hon. Secretary.I accede to your request with the utmost pleasure.
One of the most painful,let me assure you, and at the same time, one of the most frequently recurring, reflections that, as an Irish man, I am compelled to make in connection with the present aspect of things in this country, is derived from the ugly and irritating fact, that we are daily importing goods, which we cannot help doing, since she has practically strangled our own manufacturing appliances, but, together with her fashions, her accents, her vicious literature, her music, her dances and her manifold mannerisms, her games also, and her pastimes, to the utter discredit of our own grand national sports and to the sore humiliation of every genuine son and daughter of the old land.
Ball-playing, hurling, football-kicking according to Irish rules, 'casting', leaping in various ways, wrestling, handy-grips, top-pegging, leap-frog, rounders, tip-in -the-hat, and all such favourite exercises and amusements amongst men and boys may now be said to be not only dead and buried, but in several localities to be entirely forgotten and unknown.And what have we got in their stead? We have got such foreign and fantastic field sports as lawn tennis, polo, croquet, cricket and the like - very excellent, I believe, and health-giving exercise in their way, still not racy of the soil, but rather alien, on the contrary, to it, as are indeed, for the most part, the men and women who first imported, and continue

to patronise them.
And, unfortunately, it is not our national sports alone that are held in dishonour and are dying out, but even the most suggestive national celebrations are being gradually effaced and extinguished, one after another as well.Who hears now of snap-apple night, pan-cake night, or bon-fire night? They are all things of the past, too vulgar to be spoken of except in ridicule by the degenerate dandies of the day.No doubt, there is something pleasing ti the eye in the get-up of a modern man, who arrayed in light attire, with parti-coloured cap on and a racquet in hand, making his way, with or without a companion, to the tennis ground.But for my part, I should vastly prefer to behold, or think of, the useful athletes whom I used to see in my early days at fair and pattern, bereft of shoes and coat, and thus prepared to play at handball, to fly over any numbers of horses, to throw the 'sledge', or 'winding stone', and to test each other's metal and activity by the trying ordeal of 'three leaps' or a 'hop', step and jump'.
Indeed if we continue travelling for the next score years in the same direction that we have been going for some time past, condemning the sports that were practiced by our forefathers, effacing our national features as though we were ashamed of them, and putting on, with England's stuffs and broadcloths, her master habits and such other effeminate follies as she may recommend, we had better at once, and publicly, abjure our nationality, clap our hands for joy at the sight of the Union Jack, and place 'England's bloody red' exultantly above the green.
Deprecating as I do any such dire and disgraceful consummation, and seeing it in your society of athletes something altogether opposing to it, I shall be happy to do all for it that I can, and authorise you now formally to place my name on the roll of your patrons.
In conclusion, I earnestly hope that our national journals will not distain in future to give suitable notices of these Irish sports and pastimes which your Society means to patronise and promote, and that the masters and pupils of our Irish Colleges will not henceforth exclude from their athletic programmes such manly exercises as I have just referred to and commemorated.

I remain, my very dear Sir,
Your very faithful servant
T.W Croke
Archbishop of Cashel.

Reprinted from GAA Official Guide, 1995; pp. 89-91

APPENDIX 2
DISTRIBUTION OF GAELIC LEARNERS WITHIN SCOTLAND

Based on CNG-commissioned Report by John M.K Galloway; 'Estimation of the Number and Distribution of Adult Learners of Gaelic'; October, 1995.

TABLE 1:

Estimated Scottish distribution of adult Gaelic Learners, sometime active mid-1993 to mid-1995.

New Council Areas	Estimated total Learners
Aberdeenshire Council	378
Angus Council	451
Argyll & Bute Council	435
Borders Council	72
City of Aberdeen Council	572
City of Dundee Council	81
City of Edinburgh Council	612
Dumfries & Galloway Council	72
Highland Council	2269
Moray Council	282
Perthshire & Kinross Council	242
Stirling Council	153
Western Isles Council	588
Other Areas	
Glasgow postcode area (see Note 1)	1038
Lothians - excluding Edinburgh	411
Stirlingshire	274
Total	7930

Notes

1. The only information from this source for the present Strathclyde Region was for Argyll & Bute and 'Glasgow'. The latter was explained as the Glasgow postcode area, but this left several areas, such as Ayrshire, unaccounted for. However, in the current absence of further information, the given distribution has to suffice.

2. It was not possible to make any valid analysis of the council area totals to show the local numbers at different levels of learning. However, an approximate national division would be:
Beginners 12%; Lower Intermediate 56%; Upper Intermediate 23%; Advanced 9%

TABLE 2

Estimated World-wide Distribution of Adult Scottish Gaelic Learners, sometime active during the period mid-1993 to mid-1995.

Australia	600
Belgium	15
Canada	500
Southern Ireland	80
Northern Ireland	60
England	1600
Wales	50
Scotland	7930
Estonia	1
Finland	1
France	10
Germany	50
Hungary	1
Netherlands	10
New Zealand	125
South Africa	2
Sweden	3
Switzerland	1
USA	12000
Total	23039

Note : The information received indicated that most overseas learners are at the Beginner or Lower Intermediate levels.

APPENDIX 3

COMBINED GCE ADVANCED AND ORDINARY LEVEL ENTRIES IN NORTHERN IRELAND

Figures cited in G Maguire Our Own Language: An Irish Initiative (1991), p. 46.

	Irish	French	German	Spanish
1960	1163	4350	599	97
1965	1624	7402	1114	357
1970	2348	8859	1287	903
1975	2124	8904	1330	1133
1980	2065	9799	1341	1215
1985	1991	9226	1118	1248

Note In 1996 (See Chap. 5, Footnote 44), a record 2,215 candidates entered for GCSE (the O'Level successor) Irish in Northern Ireland.

APPENDIX 4

BOARD OF DIRECTORS OF LA NEWSPAPER, BELFAST

Gearoid O'Caireallain Founder Editor and current President Conradh na Gaelige
Eoghan O'Neill Current Editor and Gaeilgeoir activist.
Aine Ni Gearailt Longstanding community Gaeilgeoir and Gaelic bookshop proprietor.
Brendan O'Mearain Leading Belfast Gaeilgeoir activist
Seamus MacSeain Active Belfast Gaeilgeoir and current proprietor of Andersonstown News, Belfast; a Nationalist community paper.

Note: Information provided by Gearoid O'Caireallain in discussion, 21st July, 1997

APPENDIX 5
GAELIC MEDIUM EDUCATION UNITS IN SCOTTISH PRIMARY SCHOOLS: PUPIL NUMBERS 1995-96

Figures compiled by Gaelic Department, University of Strathclyde, Jordanhill Campus, Glasgow: supplied and amended by D.J Maciver.

SCHOOL	REGION	PUPIL NUMBERS, 1995-96
Aberdeen: Gilcomstoun	GRC	40
Acharacle	HRC	26
Aird, Lewis	CNE	19
Airidhantuim, Lewis	CNE	16
Back, Lewis	CNE	38
Balivanich, Benbecula	CNE	20
Barvas, Lewis	CNE	24
Bernera, Lewis	CNE	4
Bishopbriggs, Meadowburn	SRC	59
Browmore, Islay	SRC	25
Breasclete, Lewis	CNE	36
Broadford, Skye	HRC	35
Carinish, North Uist	CNE	45
Carloway, Lewis	CNE	22
Castlebay, Barra	CNE	25
Central, Inverness	HRC	112
Cornaigmore, Tiree	SRC	36
Daliburgh, South Uist	CNE	59
Dingwall	HRC	23
Dunskelar, North Uist	CNE	2
Dunvegan, Skye	HRC	22
East Kilbride, Mount Cameron	SRC	39
Edinburgh, Tollcross	LRC	51
Forfar, Kirkriggs	TRC	4
Fort William	HRC	9
Gairloch	HRC	8
Glasgow, Sir John Maxwell	SRC	102

SCHOOL	REGION	PUPIL NUMBERS, 1995-96
Lochdar, South Uist	CNE	48
Knockianduie, Lewis	CNE	8
Laxdale, Lewis	CNE	32
Leverburgh, Harris	CNE	15
Lionel, Ness	CNE	8
Lochcarron	HRC	12
Morar, Lady Loval	HRC	5
Newtonmore	HRC	16
Paible, North Uist	CNE	36
Perth, Northern District	TRC	14
Peterhead,Dales Park	GRC	3
Plockton	HRC	27
Portree, Skye	HRC	119
Shawbost, Lewis	CNE	6
Sleat, Skye	HRC	24
Staffin Skye	HRC	22
Stoneybridge, South Uist	CNE	21
Stornoway, Lewis	CNE	43
Tain Craighill	HRC	33
Tarbert, Harris	CNE	19
Tongue, Sutherland	HRC	10
Uig, Lewis	CNE	9
Ullapool	HRC	25
Sandwick, Lewis	CNE	5
TOTAL		1461

Note The following glossary explains the abbreviations of the various Scottish Councils:

CNE Comhairle Nan Eilean (Western Isles Council)
GRC Grampian Regional Council
HRC Highlands Regional Council
LRC Lothians Regional Council
SRC Strathclyde Regional Council
TRC Tayside Regional Council.

APPENDIX 6
SCOTTISH GAELIC PRE-SCHOOL GROUP LOCATIONS

Figures supplied in Memorandum from Keith Scammell, Secretary Comhairle Nan Sgoiltean Araich, Inverness, 8th July, 1997

WESTERN ISLES

Lewis: Barvas, Breasclete, Carloway, Stornoway, Back, Uig, Great Bernera,Ness, Borve, Laxay, Knock, Tong, Sandwick,Balallan, Bayble, Knockandue. Total 16
Harris: Tarbert, Scalpay, Leverburgh. Total 3
North Uist: Berneray, Carinish, Lochmaddy, Paible, Dunskellar Total 5
South Uist: Daliburgh, Stoneybridge, Eochar. Total 3
Barra: Eriskay, Castlebay. Total 2

HIGHLANDS:

Skye & Lochalsh: Dunvegan, Staffin, Portree, Broadford, Sleat, Kilmuir, Plockton, Achmore. Total 8
Ross-shire: Gairloch, Ullapool, Lochcarron, Kinlochbervie, Lochinver, Tain,Dingwall Total 7
Inverness, Nairn & Badenoch: Inverness , Kinmylies, Inverness Central, Newtonmore, Nairn. Total 4
Lochaber: Fort William, Acharacle, Morar, Isle of Eigg, Roybridge, Kinlochleven. Total 6
Caithness & Sutherland: Melness, Thurso. Total 2

SOUTH STRATHCLYDE:

Bishopsbriggs, Partick (Glasgow), Pollockshields (Glasgow), East Kilbride, Cumbernauld, Airdrie, Kilmarnock, Denny. Total 8

ARGYLL:

Tiree, Tobermory (Mull), Salen (Mull), Oban, Bowmore (Islay), Campbelltown, Lismore. Total 7

ABERDEEN CITY & SHIRE:

Aberdeen, Old Deer, Peterhead, Ellon. Total 4

STIRLING:

Dunblane. Total 1

PERTH, KINROSS& ANGUKS:

Perth, Forfar, Montrose, Aberfeldy. Total 4

LOTHIAN & FYFE:

Edinburgh, Dunfermline. Total 2

LOCAL EDUCATION AUTHORITY NURSERY SCHOOLS:

Balivanich (Western Isles), Edinburgh, Inverness, Portree. Total 4

Note: At the time of writing, pupil numbers per-group were not available.

APPENDIX 7
IRISH MEDIUM NURSERY EDUCATION
NAISCOILEANNA

Information supplied by Cathail O'Donnaighle, Development Officer, An Chomhairle don Oideachas Lan-Ghaeilge/Gaeloiliuint, (Council for Irish Medium Education, Belfast); 1st July 1997.

Ainm	Bunaithe	Daltai
1. Naiscoil Bhreandain, A/Town (belfast)	1971	55
2. Nai-aonad Bhreandain, A/town	1985	50
3. Naiscoil Ard Eoin, Ardoyne (Belfast)	1984	10
4. Naiscoil na Rinne, Derry	1985	18
5. Naiscoil na bhFal, Falls (Belfast)	1985	40
6. Nai-aonad na bhfal, Falls	1991	40
7. Na an tSleibhe Dhuibh, Whiterock (Belfast)	1994	24
8. N.Bharr an Chluanai, Whiterock (Belfast)	1988	13
9. Naionra na Mona, gort na Mona (Belfast)	1990	13
10. Na Bheann Mhadagain, Ardoyne (Belfast)	1994	21
11. Naiscoil an Loiste Uir, New Lodge (Belfast)	1989	10
12. Naiscoil an Droichid, Lower Ormeau (Belfast)	1990	10
13. Naiscoil an Fuiseoige, Twinbrook (Belfast)	1987	33
14. Naiscoil Dhun Lathai,Dunloy, Co.Antrim	1995	15
15. Naiscoil Dhun Padraig, Downpatrick, Co. Down	1995	15
16. Naiscoil an Iuir, Newry, Co. Down	1986	26
17. Naiscoil Charn tochair, Maghera, Co. Derry	1992	5
18. Naiscoil Luraigh, Maghera	1994	10
19. Naiscoil Ard Mhacha, Armagh	1989	24
20. Naiscoil Cholm Cille, Derry	1987	14
21. Naiscoil Ros an Bhile, Derry	1988	21
22. Naiscoil an tStratha Bain, Strabane, Co. tyrone	1994	12
23. N. Both Domhnaigh, Gortin, Co. Tyrone	1996	14
24. Naiscoil an Chreagain, Derry	1996	16
25. Naiscoil Neachtain, Dungiven, Co. Derry	1996	18
26. Naiscoil Chamlinne, Crumlin, Co. Antrim	1996	8
27. N. Dhun Geanainn, Dungannon,Co. Tyrone	1996	23
28. N. Inis Ceithleann, Enniskillen, Co. Fermanagh	1997	10
29. N. na Bhanna, Portadown, Co. Armagh	1997	10
30. N. Ui Neill, Coalisland, Co. Tyrone	1995	22
31. N. Uachtar Tire, castlewellan, Co. Down	1997	18
32. N. Chois Locha, Lurgan, Co. Armagh	1997	20
33. N. Mhig Rabhartaigh, Derry	1997	10
34. N. Chamlocha, Camlough, Co. Armagh	1997	10
35. N. an Chaisleain, Castlederg, Co. Tyrone	1997	9
	Total	672

APPENDIX 8
IRISH MEDIUM PRIMARY EDUCATION

Names of Bunscoileanna throughout Northern Ireland, plus dates established and numbers of pupils for 1997-98.

Information supplied by Cathail O'Donnaighle, Gaeloiliuint, in Memorandum, 1st July, 1997.

Ainm	Bunaithe	Daltai
1. Bunscoil Phobal Feirste, Andersonstown,Belfast.	1971	350+
2. Bunscoil Cholm Cille, Derry.	1985	226+
3. Gaelscoil na bhFal, Lower Falls, Belfast	1987	230+
4. Bunscoil an Iuir, Newry, Co. Down.	1987	57+
5. Bunscoil na Fuiseoige, Twinbrook, Belfast	1990	72+
6. Bunscoil an tSleibhe Dhuibh, Whiterock, Belfast.	1991	77+
7. Bunscoil Luraigh, Maghera, Co Derry.	1991	21
8. Bunscoil Bheann Mhadagain, Ardoyne, Belfast.	1994	64+
9. Bunscoil Ui Neill, Coalisland, Co Tyrone	1995	20
10. Bunscoil Ard Mhaca, Armagh.	1995	33+
11. Bunscoil Dhal Riada, Dunloy, Co Antrim.	1996	12
12. Bunscoil an Droichid, Lower Ormeau, Belfast.	1996	36
13. Gaelscoil an tSratha Bain, Strabane, Co Tyrone.	1997	7
14. Gaelscoil Dhun Padraig, Downpatrick Co Down.	1997	8
	Total	1,213

Note Bunscoileanna in receipt of assistance from the Northern Ireland Department of Education, re. Maintained Status, are marked with an +.